A HISTORY OF
SELLY OAK HOSPITAL

A HISTORY OF

SELLY OAK HOSPITAL

VALERIE ARTHUR

BREWIN BOOKS

BREWIN BOOKS
56 Alcester Road,
Studley,
Warwickshire,
B80 7LG
www.brewinbooks.com

Published by Brewin Books 2015

© 2015 Valerie Arthur

The author has asserted her rights in accordance with the Copyright, Designs and Patents Act 1988 to be identified as the author of this work.

All rights reserved. No part of this publication may be reproduced, stored in a retrieval system, or transmitted in any form or by any means, electronic, mechanical, photocopying, recording or otherwise, without the prior permission in writing of the publisher and the copyright owners, or as expressly permitted by law, or under terms agreed with the appropriate reprographics rights organization. Enquiries concerning reproduction outside the terms stated here should be sent to the publishers at the UK address printed on this page.

The publisher makes no representation, express or implied, with regard to the accuracy of the information contained in this book and cannot accept any legal responsibility for any errors or omissions that may be made.

A CIP catalogue record for this book is available from the British Library.

978-1-85858-533-8

Printed and bound in Great Britain
by 4edge Limited.

Contents

Acknowledgements 7
Foreword 9
Preface 11

Part One: 1872-1948

Introduction 13
Chapter 1   King's Norton Poor Law Union 17
Chapter 2   King's Norton Union Workhouse 30
Chapter 3   Life in The Workhouse 38
Chapter 4   The Casual (Vagrants') Wards 49
Chapter 5   King's Norton Union Workhouse Infirmary 57

Part Two: 1948-2012

Introduction 71
Chapter 6   Selly Oak Hospital 73
Chapter 7   Memories of Selly Oak Hospital 85
Chapter 8   Conclusion 134

Timeline 136
Sources 138
Index 142

Acknowledgements

My sincere thanks go to the following people without whose help this book would not have been possible.

Paddy Andrews, who kindly loaned me her father's King's Norton Union Workhouse Handbooks. Without those two small volumes this project would have lacked much.

Jane Tovey of the Medical Illustration Department, University Hospitals Birmingham NHS Foundation Trust for her invaluable help throughout this project.

Mary Harding who took an interest and kindly loaned me postcards from her collection to be reproduced in the book.

Dr. Ronald Jubb for his unstinting support, photographs and writing the foreword to this book.

Ruth Clarke for her help, photographs and just for listening and reminding me of forgotten events and facts.

David Rosser who spent many hours checking and advising me on the final manuscript.

Richard Daniels for the photographs he took one day, long ago, in 2004.

Louise Adamson for her help with the plans of the workhouse and infirmary.

My grateful thanks go to the following people for sharing their memories:

Jennifer Bates	Sheila Cochrane	Madeline Stafford	Joan Teasedale
Edith Elford	Margaret Godfrey	Frank Woolley	Irene Underwood
Jill Stokes	Doreen Smedley	Jenny Eley	
Iris Thompson	Marion Wood	Maud McCann	
Daisie Williams	Grace Harkin	Dot Stokes	

Foreword
By Dr. Ronald Jubb

Since 2012, Selly Oak Hospital, Birmingham, has sheltered behind a two metre high vandal-proof fence. The clinical services have moved a mile to the new Queen Elizabeth Hospital, in Edgbaston. The original hospital, built in 1897, is due for demolition and the future of the older buildings, part of the original workhouse, remains uncertain. These Victorian monuments have served the people of South Birmingham and beyond for the past one hundred and forty years but in a few years' times there will be little physical evidence left. The future might have been very different if the plans for Selly Oak Hospital, in the 1960s, had come to fruition. A history of this Birmingham institution is timely, before the loss of the bricks and mortar and the personal memories.

I first met Valerie Arthur when I joined the staff of Selly Oak Hospital in 1984 as a consultant rheumatologist to lead a newly formed Arthritis Centre. This was at a time of growth of specialist services at the hospital. Valerie had been appointed as a research nurse in the department and for the next two decades we worked together, caring for the many patients with arthritis that poured into the hospital.

As an outsider to Birmingham, it took me some time to understand why elderly patients were often reluctant to come into hospital. The geriatric ward that awaited them had been, until the formation of the NHS, part of Selly Oak House, the successor to the workhouse. Physiotherapy was in the main workhouse building, our office in the old matron's home and our ward in the original infirmary of the workhouse. Latterly, my office was moved to the building on Oak Tree Lane, which was erected to cater for the tramps. My room was sandwiched between two entrances, one for the men and the other for the women. I often thought of those who had passed through the doors, everyone with a harrowing tale.

Valerie has taken up the challenge of writing a history of this important Birmingham landmark. She has previously written a biography of her mother and the history of Great Yarmouth Hospital. As well as sorting through extensive archive material, she has been able to gather many first hand accounts of the hospital dating back to the 1920s. This provides a fascinating window into the everyday life of the hospital. Briefly, I tried to help Valerie after she had retired. I had been told that there were two boxes of records in the cellar under my office. Unfortunately, this was not the case and Valerie has had to search far and wide to put together this scholarly work on an important part of the history of Birmingham.

There is an irony that the extremes of the Victorian industrial revolution existed side by side in south Birmingham, the Selly Oak Workhouse catering for the destitute and fall-out from the industrial revolution and the model village and chocolate factory across the road with its exemplary working practices, built by George Cadbury.

Valerie gives us both the chronology of the birth and growth of the hospital from the Poor Laws that led directly to the formation of the workhouses and also an insight into the human experiences. There is a fascinating chapter on the trials and tribulations of the tramps and another on personal reflections of the hospital from interviews with staff, patients and local residents. The work is illustrated throughout with a fine collection of pictures.

The book is a must for anyone who has worked at Selly Oak Hospital, all who have been treated there, the many visitors to the hospital and the local residents who have lived in the shadow of this popular hospital. Those with an interest in the history of Birmingham, the Victorian workhouses or the evolution of hospital care over the past one hundred and fifty years will find much to interest and enjoy.

I strongly recommend this important addition to local history.

Preface

This book has been written to record the history of Selly Oak Hospital; a place for the care of the sick and needy for nearly one hundred and forty years. The first buildings were those of the King's Norton Union Workhouse, which was opened in 1872 and the King's Norton Union Workhouse Infirmary which was built next to the workhouse and opened in 1897. These two establishments eventually became Selly Oak Hospital. In 2010, the hospital was closed and services were moved to the Queen Elizabeth Hospital in Edgbaston.

At the time of closure, there was a hotch potch of buildings of different ages, shapes and sizes on the extensive site. At the western end, stood the out-patient department and at the eastern end was the main hospital block. In between were green spaces and various red brick buildings, many with newer extensions, besides numerous prefabricated cabins, car parks, pedestrian ramps, and information signs. Despite this it was still possible to detect the original layout of the workhouse and infirmary. The fine Victorian buildings still stood proudly; they had served their purpose and weathered the years well and were a reminder of how the care for the sick and poor had evolved since the latter part of the nineteenth century.

I worked, as a nurse, at Selly Oak Hospital for over twenty years and often wondered about the history behind the buildings. Some of my patients told me stories of the days when part of the hospital was a workhouse and I decided to learn more. My research took me to Birmingham Central Library where I found some historical background in the city archives. Then a lady whose father had worked for the King's Norton Poor Law Union lent me two small workhouse handbooks which proved so interesting and useful that I was spurred on to discover more. Former and current members of hospital staff and local residents generously and enthusiastically shared their memories, photographs and ephemera and so enabled me to build a more detailed picture of the hospital.

The result is this book, which I hope you will enjoy as much as I have enjoyed researching and writing it.

Part One
1872-1948

Introduction

The Industrial Revolution of the eighteenth and nineteenth centuries made Great Britain one of the wealthiest countries in the world. However, the increase in wealth did not extend to the majority of the burgeoning population, and pauperism a state of poverty and destitution, was common.

As early as the fourteenth century there had been concern for the plight of the poor. Some parishes provided relief in the form of funds or accommodation but this was not always a reliable system and paupers had to seek help from family and friends, or from religious and charitable institutions. The dissolution of the monasteries, during the reign of Henry VIII, removed a vital source of food, shelter and medical care for the poor and caused a great deal of hardship. In an attempt to address this problem several acts of parliament were passed, which were finally amalgamated into the Elizabethan Poor Law of 1601. This law, known as the Old Poor Law, became the foundation of welfare provision in this country for the next three centuries.

The Old Poor Law 1601

The Old Poor Law was administered by overseers of the poor appointed by each parish. Funds, known as poor relief, were raised from taxes levied on property, and were made available to those who were able to work until they found employment. The deserving poor, those unable to work due to old age or ill health, were maintained in parish-houses, or almshouses. Poor relief was only given to those who were born in a particular parish. Paupers residing in a parish but not born there, were removed to their native parish, and if this was unknown, to the last place where they had resided for at least a year. Whether a person was native to a parish, and if not, their removal often caused families to be split up with subsequent deprivation, further poverty and despair.

The Act of Settlement and Removal 1662
Unfortunately this law, which was passed to mitigate the problems associated with settlement, did not really work, and became infamous over the next two and half centuries for the controversy and distress it caused. After 1662, a newcomer to a parish was given the right to settlement provided he had lived there unchallenged for forty days, or if he rented a property worth £10 a year, thereby proving that he had sufficient funds and would not be likely to make a charge on the parish. As the rent of an average labourer's cottage, at that time, was fifty shillings or less per annum, this clearly meant that many paupers were at risk of being removed.

An amendment to the Act, in 1692, granted settlement to certain groups of people: those who paid rates, held parish office, were apprenticed or had been employed in a particular parish for a year. In other words, those who would not be a burden on the tax payer. Many employers, who paid taxes for local poor relief, circumvented this amendment by engaging workers for three hundred and sixty four days rather than a whole year, which meant that their employees could not claim settlement rights. However, one improvement brought about by this amendment, was that women, through marriage, were granted settlement in their husband's parish, thus ensuring that spouses were not separated even if they came from different parishes.

It no longer became necessary for families to be split up, providing that any children were born legitimately to the couple. Illegitimate children took the settlement of their birthplace, which might not necessarily be that of their parents and they could therefore, be separated from them.

In 1795, a further amendment to the Act of Settlement sought to address the plight of the sick poor following public outrage, which had been provoked by the publication of several reports of paupers being removed to their place of settlement whilst seriously ill. The amendment permitted justices of the peace to defer the removal of a sick person until they were fit to travel. The settlement and removal of paupers continued into the 20th century. Indeed it was reported that in 1907 more than 12,000 people had been subjected to this treatment. Removal itself was costly, but was nothing compared to the large sums of money run up in legal fees for disputed settlement cases. In terms of human misery the cost was immeasurable. Despite constant criticism, no action was taken to repeal the Law of Settlement and Removal, even though in 1847, both Houses of Parliament

Introduction

agreed that it produced hardship and impeded the free circulation of labour by tying the poor to their place of birth.

Workhouses to shelter the poor were commonplace. They were favoured by rate payers as being less costly than outdoor relief, a weekly system of maintenance which enabled people to remain in their own homes. Throughout the country reports abounded of badly run workhouses and the terrible conditions endured by the inmates. In 1784, the cost of poor relief was approximately £2 million. This had risen to approximately £7 million by 1832, as pauperism increased.

The reasons for this were the gradual enclosure of common land which deprived many cottagers of the means to graze their animals and grow their own food, and unemployment created by increasing mechanisation compounded the problem. Agricultural machinery replaced many farm workers and large, complicated machines in factories replaced piece work, such as weaving, lace, glove and stocking making, traditionally the work of women in their cottages. The subsequent lack of employment in the countryside encouraged a population drift to the factories of the rapidly expanding cities and towns in the Midlands and North of England. The rising cost of providing poor relief became a national problem and a Commission of Inquiry was set up by the government in 1832. Twenty-six assistant commissioners visited three thousand of the fifteen thousand parishes in England and Wales. They amassed thirteen volumes of evidence with a total of nearly eight thousand pages.

The Poor Law Amendment Act 1834 (The New Poor Law)

The report from these documents resulted in the Poor Law Amendment Act of 1834, which set out that all able-bodied persons who sought poor relief would be admitted, with their families, into the workhouse. Between 1834 and 1883 five hundred and fifty four new workhouses were built throughout England and Wales. Three poor law commissioners in London supervised the amalgamation of parishes into poor law unions. Each union had an elected board of guardians, made up of local worthies, who gave their services voluntarily. Central supervision from London ensured that nationally the New Poor Law was administered uniformly, but ultimately local boards dictated how humanely the rules and regulations from London were interpreted. Interestingly there was no official definition of what 'able-bodied' meant. This inevitably resulted in some disparity in the treatment of the poor in different unions.

The basis of the new law was to deter people from seeking relief. Generally it was assumed that the able-bodied poor could find work and if they didn't they were feckless idlers, who should be forced to work within the confines of the workhouse. To ensure this, outdoor relief was denied under the new act. Within the workhouse paupers endured harsh treatment and conditions; they were subject to strict rules and regulations and husbands and wives were separated from each other and their children.

In the late nineteenth and early twentieth centuries the authorities gradually softened their approach, as it became apparent that workhouses were refuges for those unable to work or even to fend for themselves, such as orphans, the elderly, widows with young children, the chronically sick and lunatics. In time, most unions set up separate institutions for children and lunatics and eventually workhouses accommodated mainly the chronic sick and elderly, often with a separate infirmary for the acute sick.

It also began to be accepted that the plight of the able-bodied poor was not necessarily due to a desire for a life of idleness, but more importantly because there was no work. This was recognised by Joseph Chamberlain in 1886, who as President of the Local Government Board, sent out a circular stating 'that men unemployed through no fault of their own should be spared the stigma of pauperism and be found jobs in large scale public works'. In London a survey undertaken by Charles Booth between 1889 and 1903, found that most people were poor due to no fault of their own, and that of those who reached the age of seventy, one in three sought poor relief.

In 1905, a Royal Commission looked at the whole structure of poor relief, but could reach no agreement on how best to deal with the problem of the poor; the majority favoured retaining the Poor Law, but with reforms, whilst the minority wanted it scrapped. What the Commission did reveal, in a report from the Local Government Board in 1907, was that 47.7 per 1,000 persons (excluding casual paupers and lunatics) were given poor relief and that the total cost to the nation was £14.5 million every year. From 1908, with the introduction of old age pensions and in 1911 the National Insurance state scheme, the numbers admitted to the workhouse began to drop. During the First World War the lowest number of paupers for two centuries was reported.

The end of the Poor Law came in 1930, when local government boards took over the running of all poor law institutions, although it wasn't until 1948, and the introduction of the National Health Service, that the administration of hospitals and other former workhouse institutions began to change. The National Assistance Act of 1948, ended three hundred years of poor relief based upon destitution by allowing those in need to seek relief without having to enter a workhouse or similar institution. Admission into these grim places had always carried a stigma, which inevitably became attached to the many workhouse institutions that eventually became National Health Service hospitals.

Chapter 1

King's Norton Poor Law Union

As a result of the Poor Law Amendment Act of 1834, parishes throughout the country were amalgamated into large poor law unions. In 1836, the King's Norton Poor Law Union was formed from the five parishes of Harborne (including Smethwick), Edgbaston, King's Norton, Northfield (including Selly Oak) and Beoley (including Balsall Heath, Moseley, King's Heath, Wythall and Stirchley). These parishes lay, at that time, within the three counties of Warwickshire, Worcestershire and Staffordshire. The King's Norton Poor Law Union was responsible for workhouses in each of the five parishes. Following a national trend these smaller workhouses were replaced, in 1872, by a large one at Selly Oak.

Each poor law union was managed by a board of guardians made up of voluntary members who were elected by local ratepayers. The responsibilities of each board were diverse and far-reaching and show the beginnings of the present day welfare system and local council administration. Central supervision by the Poor Law Commissioners in London ensured uniformity throughout the country, although at a local level rules and regulations were often interpreted differently with some boards meting out harsher treatment than others. Each board had to provide not only for the able-bodied poor in their union, but also for those who were poor by default, such as lunatics, orphans, the aged and the infirm. Other duties of the boards were the valuation of property, the collection of rates, public health, education and the registration of births, deaths and marriages.

Positions on the boards were contested annually. Some guardians remained in post for years, perhaps with an eye to financial gain, or with fixed views about the way in which paupers should be treated, or with the intention of reducing the tax rate to keep local tax payers happy. Initially there were few women guardians, but eventually the number of women taking on the role rose from 50 in 1885 to 1,300 by 1909. This was in part due to the qualifications for guardianship being extended to include persons having the means to rent a property worth £40 or more per annum, who had lived in a parish for at least a year, or were entitled to vote (i.e male householders over the age of 21 years).

It is clear that the twentieth century brought about a more kindly approach to poverty, and workhouse conditions, which generally had been extremely harsh and cruel, gradually improved. Eventually there was reform of the poor law system and this paved the way for the introduction of the National Health and Social Security Services.

The King's Norton Poor Law Union at the beginning of the twentieth century

Some idea of how the poor law functioned in the King's Norton Union can be discovered by examining the official handbooks of the period. By then conditions were better than previously although the workhouse regime was still harsh by today's standards.

The King's Norton Union was divided into three districts made up of local parishes: the northern (Smethwick), central (Balsall Heath, Harborne and Edgbaston) and southern (Moseley, Selly Oak, Northfield, Bartley Green, Stirchley, King's Heath, Wythall, Beoley and King's Norton). Each parish was represented by at least one guardian (Edgbaston) whilst several guardians stood for the larger districts (Smethwick and King's Norton). The union was managed centrally from the workhouse at Selly Oak with more local venues in each parish for the distribution of outdoor relief. Two very different examples show that the union provided for both an urban and a rural population: in Harborne where the population was 10,113 (according to the census of 1901), outdoor relief was given from the Free Library in the High Street every Tuesday from 12 to 12.30 and every Thursday 1.45 to 2.30pm; whilst in the parish of Beoley, with a population of 565, it could be obtained from Mrs. Wheeler's, Seafield Lane, on Fridays at about 12.30pm.

In 1902, there were twenty-eight members on the King's Norton Union Board of Guardians, three of whom were women. The Reverend George Astbury, Vicar of Smethwick, was Chairman and Alderman Thomas Bayliss JP of Northfield, the vice-chairman. Three previous chairmen, Robert Mynors, John Rutter and T.S. Fallows, had held their posts for twenty, eighteen and fourteen years respectively, demonstrating that chairmen often remained in office for long periods of time. The board met on the second and fourth Wednesday of every month, at 11 am, in the Board Room of the Union Buildings on Raddle Barn Lane (now Raddlebarn Road). The Finance and Assessment committees, each made up of ten members, none of whom were women, met at the workhouse prior to the board meetings. On Tuesdays, in the weeks preceding the board meetings, the committee responsible for visiting the workhouse and infirmary, of which two members were women, met at 2.45pm.

Responsibilities of the Board of Guardians
1. Provision for the poor – outdoor relief

The main responsibility of the guardians was to provide relief for the poor. Although the Poor Law Amendment Act of 1834 dictated that the able-bodied poor should be accommodated within the workhouse, as the number of people seeking relief rose and workhouses became home to the chronic sick and elderly, it became common for outdoor rather than indoor relief to be given. In the King's Norton Union, three local relieving officers from each of the districts gathered evidence about applicants, which they then produced at the weekly board meetings, when it was decided whether outdoor or indoor relief would be granted.

Twenty four overseers of the poor were appointed by local justices of the peace to serve for a year from Lady Day (25th March). Their main duties were to collect rates and to give outdoor relief. They were also responsible for making sure that those not entitled to poor relief did not receive funds. They had to find the fathers of illegitimate children so that the cost of care could be charged to the father's parish. Another part of their job was to make sure that casual paupers (tramps) were removed to their parish of settlement.

As shown in **Table 1**, the rules and regulations for those who did not qualify to receive outdoor relief reflect the strict moral code of the day. Having illegitimate children and lavish spending of more than £5 on a husband's funeral expenses were two of several reasons to refuse outdoor relief for women. A more charitable approach was adopted for those without obvious means of support, such as women living apart from their husbands, the aged and infirm with no family support and those living in poor conditions. In those days families generally lived in the same area, and it was expected that the old would be cared for by their immediate family. Indeed in cases where outdoor relief was given, relatives, who were able, were legally bound to support the beneficiaries, and subsequently had to refund or could be compelled to refund the amount of relief received.

Table 1
RULES AND REGULATIONS AS TO THE ADMINISTRATION OF OUTDOOR RELIEF

> I. Relief must be assured to all, whatever the cause of destitution. The destitute must be secure against starvation.
> II. The Workhouse is prescribed as the ordinary mode of relief for all adult able-bodied paupers, male and female, and should also be adopted as far as possible for all undeserving classes of paupers.
> III. Out-door Relief should not be granted or allowed to applicants of any of the following classes:-
>   (a) Single able-bodied men.
>   (b) Single able-bodied women, with or without illegitimate children.
>   (c) Widows with illegitimate children.
>   (d) Able-bodied Widows without children or having only one child to support, except during the first six months of widowhood.
>   (e) Women who, during the twelve months prior to application, have become Widows, and who on the death of their husband have received money from a Club, Insurance Society or other sources, which in the opinion of the Board, has been lavishly spent in mourning or funeral expenses… (Note the actual burial expenses should not exceed £5).
>   (f) Persons residing with relatives where the united income of the family is sufficient for the support of all its members.
>   (g) Women living apart from their husbands with or without legitimate children.
>   (h) Aged and infirm persons residing in a room or cottage without a relative to attend them in case of necessity.
>   (i) Persons residing in any house or premises, which are in an overcrowded or insanitary condition.
>   (j) Persons who let lodgings or rooms to more than a married couple without children, or to more than one lodger.
>   (k) Persons having resident with them any woman with an illegitimate child or children, or any person of immoral habits.
>   (l) Where the total weekly earnings or income from all sources amounts, after deducting rent, to 2s 6d, per head for each person to be maintained.
>   (m) Destitute undeserving persons.
>
> *The King's Norton Union Official Handbook (1902-3)*

There were some exceptions to the rules for outdoor relief such as: sudden and urgent necessity, sickness and accident, and for the dependants of those confined to a lunatic asylum. Widows of good character could be helped and their children sent to the cottage homes. Aged, infirm persons, above the age of sixty, could receive relief if they had shown signs of thrift, were able to pay the rent on their homes and had been unable to obtain help from any charity. Frequently the term 'deserving' crops up, but what constitutes deserving is unclear and the provision of outdoor relief was probably subject to the inclination or otherwise of the relieving officers. Strict conditions were applied for the duration of relief; new cases could receive it weekly for four weeks and then subsequently for no longer than fourteen weeks. In cases of sickness, a note had to be obtained after four weeks from a medical officer. Paupers and their families who were refused outdoor relief had little choice but to apply to the workhouse for admission.

In 1902, outdoor relief given to aged and infirm married couples between 60 and 70 years of age was not more than 4s 6d and one loaf of bread a week. Married couples over the age of 70 received 5 shilling. Single persons between 60 and 70 years of age had no more than 2s 6d weekly, and those above 70 years, not more than 3 shillings. Imbeciles who lived with relatives or friends, were given no more than 3 shillings weekly. The provision for widows was not more than 1 shilling and 6 pence and one loaf of bread weekly for each child. Wives and families of men in lunatic asylums or whose husbands were soldiers, sailors or marines received not more than 1 shilling and a loaf of bread per week for each child other than the first. The emphasis on the 'not more than' suggests that the amounts specified are arbitrary and the amount actually received was decided by union officials.

The 'Evils' of Settlement

It was important to establish a person's place of birth (place of settlement) as relief could be denied to paupers if they had not been born in the union from which they were seeking help.

A comparison of the birthplaces of inmates in the King's Norton Union Workhouse in 1881 and 1901 (**Table 2**) shows one striking detail: that whilst every inmate in the 1881 census has a birthplace listed, in the 1901 census 30 are listed as birthplace 'unknown'. In 1881, half of the workhouse inmates came from outside unions but by 1901 this had risen to almost three quarters. The majority in 1901 came from nearby Birmingham, the Black Country and the West Midlands with some from Ireland, Scotland or even further away. In 1881 one inmate gave their place of birth as Bermuda and in 1901 two were born 'At Sea', one in Montreal and one in San Francisco. The upkeep of paupers born outside the union had to be borne by the ratepayers of the King's Norton Union, unless the settlement officer was able to recover the money from the unions of their birthplace; almost certainly a lost cause for those of unknown birthplace, born abroad or at sea.

Table 2
King's Norton Union Workhouse
Comparative Census Figures for 1881 and 1901
Number of Inmates born Inside and Outside King's Norton Union
(n.b. 1881 Census 1 born Bermuda, in 1901 Census
1 born San Francisco, 1 Montreal and 2 At Sea)

Year	Inmates	Unknown	King's Norton Union	Outside King's Norton Union				
				B'ham	Ireland	Scotland	Wales	Other
1881	327	none	163	30	4	3	3	124
1901	381	30	81	59	10	1	8	192

Admission to the Workhouse

For those refused outdoor relief, there were two options; complete destitution or admission to the workhouse. Many paupers, such as the mentally ill, chronic sick and orphans had little choice and, through no fault of their own, had to live out their lives in the workhouse.

Eventually during the late nineteenth century, an awareness grew of the plight of these people and many mental institutions and orphanages were founded by poor law unions.

The guardians of King's Norton Union borrowed money to build the Shenley Fields Cottage Homes, which were opened in 1887 and further extended in 1892 to accommodate children who otherwise would have ended up in the workhouse. As the name suggests, children lived in small family groups in individual cottages each with house-parents. These children had no direct association with the workhouse and so escaped, to a certain extent, the taint of pauperism. In 1910, children in the care of King's Norton Union totalled 370, of whom 260 were in the cottage homes, 31 in the workhouse, 40 in the infirmary, 5 boarded out, 25 were in certified schools and 9 in institutions catering for the blind, deaf and dumb, and epileptics. Boarded out orphans usually lived with relatives who received money for their care.

'Lunatic', 'imbecile', 'feeble minded' and 'simple' were terms used widely during the nineteenth century for anyone with a psychological condition, or conditions such as epilepsy or Down's Syndrome. There was no proper classification for those with mental illness, who were either judged to be 'lunatics' and admitted to an asylum, or 'sane', in which case they were accommodated in the workhouse, where they were either housed with other paupers or in separate lunatic wards. There was a shortage of asylums and it was cheaper to keep mentally ill paupers in the workhouse rather than pay the higher cost of their being in an asylum.

The King's Norton Poor Law Union paid £5,144 in 1894 for the maintenance of lunatics in asylums and this sum rose to £6,480 in 1901. Since there was no asylum for the mentally ill within the King's Norton Union, it is probable that some 'lunatics' were sent to the Borough Lunatic Asylum which later became All Saints Hospital. This institution, the only asylum in the Birmingham area at that time, was built in 1849 for the Birmingham Union at Winson Green beside the new Birmingham Union Workhouse which replaced the one in Lichfield Street, in the centre of Birmingham, and later became Dudley Road Hospital, and is known today as City Hospital.

In 1905, Monyhull Hall, near King's Heath, was sold to the guardians of Aston, Birmingham and King's Norton Unions and became the Monyhull Colony, a mental institution for 'epileptics and feebleminded'. This new institution removed many of the mentally ill from the workhouse to an environment where the emphasis was on self sufficiency with inmates employed on the land, gardens and within the buildings.

Public Health

The Boards of Guardians fulfilled a role later taken on by the city public health departments. At King's Norton the guardians appointed seven district medical officers, six of whom were also nominated as public vaccinators. Vaccination against smallpox was compulsory for all children of school age from 1853 until 1948 and led to the almost complete eradication of this potentially fatal disease. In 1896, within the King's Norton Union, 1,317 successful vaccinations took place; this number increased to 3,454 in 1905.

Other diseases such as tuberculosis, diphtheria, scarlet fever and typhoid were common and unless precautions were taken they swept through urban populations, especially where overcrowding, poor sanitary conditions and malnutrition were prevalent. Immunisation, improvements in housing and living conditions and an increased awareness by the general public eventually saw the end of these potentially lethal diseases, so that today we are in danger of forgetting their deadly impact. In the late nineteenth and early twentieth centuries the danger of infectious diseases, when antibiotics had yet to be discovered, could not be ignored and isolation of patients to prevent their spread was common practice.

Although there were isolation hospitals for cases of small-pox and scarlet fever, these were initially unpopular and not generally used. Eventually patients were no longer nursed at home and admission to isolation hospitals became more common. In 1871, the year of the great small-pox epidemic, the guardians of the Birmingham

Union erected wards at the Western Road Workhouse (City Hospital) for the admission of paupers with this disease. The Public Health Act of 1875 gave boards of guardians the power to build or contract hospitals for the care of those with infectious diseases. In 1883, a scarlet fever hospital was built on Lodge Road, near to the Birmingham Union workhouse, which eventually had beds for 252 patients and was also used for cases of diphtheria and typhoid fever. A small-pox epidemic in 1893 and 1894 resulted in the building, by Birmingham City Council, of a separate 'Fever' hospital at Little Bromwich, which was later to become part of the Selly Oak Group of hospitals. By the time this new hospital was completed in 1895, small-pox had ceased to be a problem, but scarlet fever had increased and by 1911 the hospital had 477 beds for convalescent cases of this disease. From 1873, patients with tuberculosis were admitted to the Birmingham and Midland Counties Sanatorium at Blackwell, near to the Lickey Hills and by 1910 this institution had beds for 100 patients. Admission cost a guinea (£1 and 1 shilling) for a fortnight in the summer or for three weeks in the winter months. Whether the isolation facilities at the Selly Oak site were sufficient to nurse very many patients with these infectious diseases is unclear, and it is possible that King's Norton Union had to finance the care of paupers at these various hospitals.

Education
Under the Elementary Education Act of 1870, poor law unions were given the power to create school boards, and to levy rates to establish and maintain elementary schools for the education of children aged between five and thirteen. There were already in existence some schools funded principally by voluntary bodies such as churches and charities. In 1891, when the city boundaries were enlarged, schools in King's Norton, Smethwick and Aston came under the control of the Birmingham City Council. School boards were dissolved in 1902 and in Birmingham, an education committee was elected to take over the responsibilities of administering both council and voluntary schools.

In 1902, ten guardians from the King's Norton Union sat on the school attendance committee which met as required. Their duties were to check the records of each of the schools within their jurisdiction and to levy penalties for absence. The aim of the authorities was to ensure that children received a regular education in the three 'R's' but it was a task fraught with many difficulties, particularly for teachers who tried to establish an orderly time table and routine to achieve this goal. At a particular disadvantage were half timers; working children who were only able to attend school in the afternoons, and the children of 'ins-and-outs', paupers who were in and out of the workhouse and by default their children.

Registration of Births, Deaths and Marriages

In 1836 two acts the Registration Act and the Marriage Act, were passed. Under these acts births, deaths and marriages had to be registered with local poor law unions and this association with the workhouse stigmatised the early days of civil registration. Prior to this records had been kept by individual parishes, but to centralise the collection of accurate records, as a resource to analyse social change and plan future policy, it was convenient to use the already established national organisation of the poor law unions. In 1902, the King's Norton Union had three registrars: Mr. Josiah Hands for the King's Norton district, Ann Baker for Edgbaston and Fred Stevens for Harborne, which included Smethwick at that time. There were specific days, times and places for registration, for instance Josiah Hands was available every Tuesday in the Board Offices, Union Buildings, Selly Oak (the workhouse), between the hours of 11.20-12.30 noon.

Assessment and Finance

All the activities of the union were paid for by local property rates, and an important function of the guardians was the assessment of the rateable value of all property within the union: land, buildings, tenements, manufactories and mills. In 1901, the total rateable value for the King's Norton Union was £862,399 which by 1906 had risen to £1,070,146. The population had also risen in that time from 187,083 to an estimate of 220,681. Rates were allocated for the following services: the poor, county, education, general district, sanitary services, parish councils, highways, drainage and other purposes. The guardians had the difficult task of finding enough money to provide for the increasing number of paupers, whilst at the same time keeping the local ratepayers happy by not increasing the rates.

(a) Rates

Rates were collected by six rate collectors, three of whom, in 1901, were also overseers of the poor.

(b) Loans

The records show that the King's Norton Union guardians regularly obtained loans. In 1869, they obtained the sum of £1,700 to purchase the land at Selly Oak for the new workhouse. This first recorded loan was for thirty years. A summary of loans in the official handbooks show the increasingly large amounts of money needed in order to build accommodation for the rising number of paupers.

(c) Insurance

All the buildings, workhouse, infirmary, nurses' homes, cottage homes and their contents were insured. In 1902, the cost of insuring the boilers was £1,500. This sum appears as a separate item in the records, presumably because repairs would have been expensive and the boilers were essential for keeping the workhouse and infirmary supplied with heat and hot water. 'Employees at the Workhouse, Infirmary and Cottage Homes' were also insured in compliance with the Employers Liability Act of 1880. The cost of this, in 1902, was £2,200, with the Ocean Accident and Guarantee Corporation Ltd.

(d) Settlement
In 1902 the Settlement and Enquiry officer, Mr. J.A. Horne, had the job of ensuring that paupers from other unions were moved back to their own parishes and that the King's Norton Union did not provide relief for them. The Statements of Receipt and Expenditure for 1902, show that money was received from other unions, and also paid out to other unions, for indoor maintenance, outdoor relief and the certification and removal of lunatics.

(e) Support of local charities
Annual subscriptions were given to sixteen local institutions and nursing charities in 1902. Voluntary hospitals such as the Queen's Hospital (later the Accident Hospital) and the General Hospital each received ten guineas (£10 10s) whilst five nursing charities were each given two guineas. Presumably this was to support these voluntary institutions which provided services for the poor of the union.

(f) Records
Officials at the workhouse, the infirmary and the cottage homes at Shenley Fields, were responsible for keeping accurate and detailed records of all activities and costs. This information was entered into leather bound books already printed out in columns for the required data. One remaining example of this, the Admission and Discharge Book for Casual Paupers February to September 1901, bears the label 'Produced by Haddon Best and Co. Printers and Publishers of Account Books Prescribed by the Local Government Board'. This particular book carries the Warwickshire Audit District Stamp for 6th February 1902. The cost of audit was £40; listed as an item of expenditure for 1903-1906. The books were examined regularly by the guardians and the results of the annual audit submitted to the Poor Law Commissioners in London for their examination and approval.

The Continued Rise of Pauperism
Pauperism was a problem that would not go away. In the Birmingham area, in the first decade of the 20th century, 23 out of every 1,000 persons was a pauper. The

average rate on property in the whole area for poor law purposes was 1 shilling and 5 pence in the pound. As can be seen in **Table 3**, both the Birmingham and Aston Unions had many more paupers than the King's Norton Union which was more rural. There was, therefore, a substantial difference between the annual cost for the maintenance and relief of city paupers in the Birmingham Union, those from the Aston Union, which included Saltley and Little Bromwich, and those in the King's Norton Union. In 1910, the annual cost in the Birmingham Union was £116,239, in the Aston Union it was £47,161, whereas in the King's Norton Union it was much lower at £25,683.

Table 3
Number of Paupers in Birmingham, Aston and King's Norton
From Birmingham Institutions (1910). The Guardians of the Poor by C.A. Carter

	Number of Paupers			
	Indoor	Outdoor	Lunatics	Totals
Birmingham	3,937	2,299	951	7,187
Aston	1,658	1,697	520	3,875
King's Norton	414	777	204	1,395
Total for the whole city	6,009	4,773	1,675	12,457

In 1911, the King's Norton Urban District was removed from the county of Worcestershire and became part of the Birmingham metropolis under the Greater Birmingham Act. The three separate unions of the city, King's Norton, Aston and Birmingham were combined and became the Birmingham Union.

Birmingham Union 1912-1930

The workhouse and infirmary at Selly Oak then became part of the Birmingham Union, and were known respectively as Selly Oak House, sometimes confusingly referred to as Selly Oak Infirmary, and Selly Oak Hospital. The Poor Law was now administered by the one authority.

Administration was centralised at offices in Edmund Street, where the board of guardians met every Wednesday. The Clerk and Solicitor to the Birmingham Union was Sir James Curtis. Dr. F. W. Ellis, the Chief Medical Officer at King's Norton Union, became its Chief Medical Officer, a post he held until 1930 when the 1929 Act of Parliament, which empowered local authorities to take over poor law institutions, came into force. The several institutions within the new enlarged Birmingham Union were managed by sub-committees, with responsibility for presenting monthly reports on administration, numbers of admissions and discharges, staff appointments and building maintenance.

Prior to this changes had been made to the way some of the institutions within the Birmingham Union operated. For instance, a labour shortage prior to the Great War 1914-1918 saw a steady decrease in the number of vagrants and this resulted, in 1913, in the closure of the tramp wards at Selly Oak House and Erdington House (formerly the Aston Union Workhouse and later Highcroft Hospital). Tramps now had to make their way to Western Road House (later Dudley Road Hospital). During the Great War, the War Office funded the conversion of Dudley Road Infirmary into a military hospital to house the huge numbers of war casualties. The inmates were rehoused in Selly Oak House and Erdington House.

Dismantling the Poor Law Unions
As the twentieth century progressed attitudes to the poor changed and the introduction of various acts of parliament slowly but surely removed the powers of the poor law unions. Since their foundation in 1834, dramatic sociological and demographic changes had made the administration of poor relief under the unions cumbersome and ineffective. Successive acts of parliament were introduced, which helped to reduce the number of people applying for relief and gradually did away with the whole poor law system.

1908 Old Age Pensions Act
Under this act an allowance, which was means tested, was given to those with incomes that were not over 12 shillings a week and who were above seventy years of age. Provision was between 1 shilling and 5 shillings a week. These pensions were paid for out of income tax and not provided by local poor law unions. Eventually this act helped to decrease the numbers of older people entering the workhouse.

1911 National Insurance Act
This act established a contributory system for wage earners which insured against sickness and unemployment. It helped some to avoid seeking poor relief and the possibility of admission to the workhouse.

1915 National Registration Act
The civil registration of births, deaths and marriages became the responsibility of local government authorities.

1925 Rating and Valuation Act
The valuation and collection of rates was removed from the poor law unions and taken over by local government authorities.

The Local Government Act 1929
The Local Government Act of 1929 abolished the poor law unions and local government authorities took over the principal duty of the boards of guardians. Public Assistance Committees became responsible for the adminstration of poor relief. 'Public Assistance' was the term used in an attempt to remove the stigma associated with poor relief and its workhouse connotations.

Birmingham City Corporation became responsible for the Birmingham Union institutions. Selly Oak House and Selly Oak Hospital were no longer known as poor law institutions, but together as Selly Oak General Hospital under the administration of the Public Health, Maternity and Welfare Committee.

Chapter 2

King's Norton Union Workhouse

In 1880 Selly Oak was described in Kelly's Directory of Birmingham, as a 'manufacturing village situated on the Bromsgrove turnpike road from Birmingham, within the larger parish of Northfield in the county of Worcestershire'. The population had increased 'owing to the erection of large works, for the manufacture of Elliot's Patent Shearing for the bottom and sides of vessels'. The ordnance survey map published in 1884 shows closely packed buildings around the triangle, formed by Bristol Road, Harborne Lane and Chapel

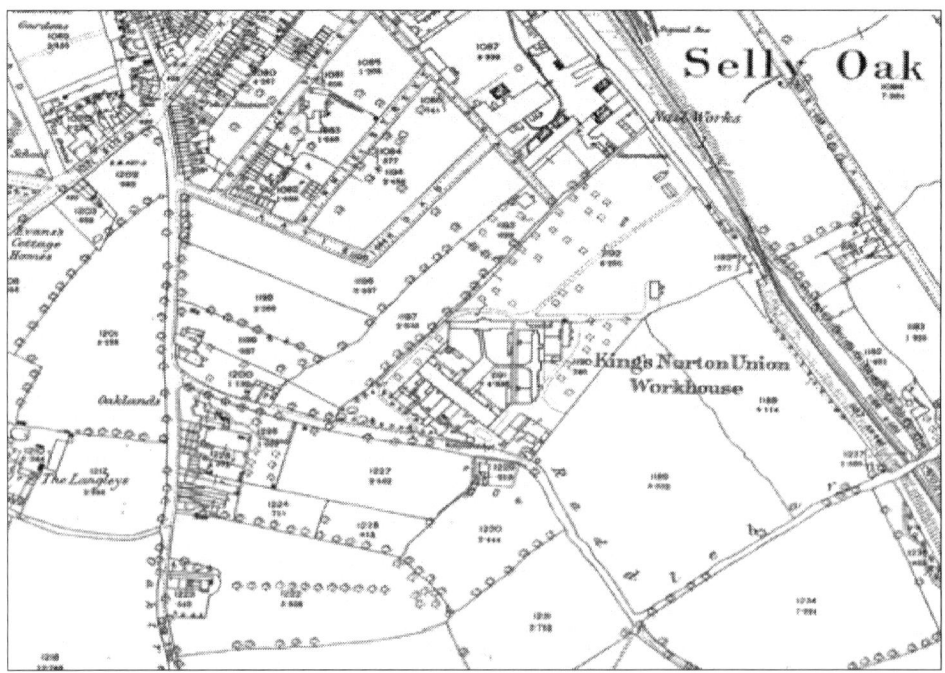

Ordnance Survey Map of King's Norton 1884.

Lane, which today is the site of a large Sainsbury's supermarket. Then there were only a few houses in Lottie and Katie Roads as the creeping urbanisation of Birmingham had yet to swallow up this predominately rural area.

The King's Norton Union Workhouse on Raddlebarn Lane, now Raddlebarn Road, was surrounded by fields. The north eastern boundary of the workhouse grounds was bordered by the Worcester and Birmingham canal, completed in 1851, and the Birmingham West Suburban Railway, opened in 1876. However, by 1904, as shown on the ordnance survey map (see page number 59), Lottie, Katie and Winnie Roads were completely built up.

Workhouse Buildings 1872

The King's Norton Union guardians purchased the land on Raddlebarn Lane for £1,700 in 1869 and the workhouse, with accommodation for 200 inmates, was opened in 1872. It was designed by Edward Holmes and cost £27,758 5s 8d. It replaced the smaller workhouse situated on the south side of King's Norton village green. The entrance building originally housed the board room and the other union offices. Behind this two storey block was a much larger three storey building

K Block built in 1872. The original front entrance has been removed and the water tower truncated. (Dr. Ronald Jubb 2013)

known later as K Block, which was built to a corridor plan with a tall, one storey wing at the back containing the workhouse kitchen and a large dining hall. A tall ornate water tower was built above the main entrance.

Workhouse design at that time incorporated the master's residence within the central section, so that the strictly segregated inmates could be observed when they were out in the exercise yards. The bay windows on either side of the main doorway would certainly have allowed a full view of the airing yards, as they were known. Corridors connected two separate pavilions to the main building: J Block to the north, probably the workhouse school and E Block to the east, possibly the infirmary. These can clearly be seen, on the ordnance survey map of 1884, along with the many walls that separated the different categories of inmates. It is possible that the two storey building, directly behind E Block, was used for tramps with the single storey building to the north east being used for infectious cases.

E Block built in 1872. Possibly the first infirmary building and the Rheumatology Department in the 1990s. (Valerie Arthur 2004)

Workhouse Buildings 1878, 1882, and 1902

In 1878, the guardians secured a loan for the 'Erection of Casual Wards for Males and Pump House'. Where the casual wards were is uncertain, but the pump house was situated close to the main entrance.

The Pump House built in 1878 from Raddlebarn Road. (Valerie Arthur 2004)

Following a national trend, the number of people admitted to the King's Norton Union workhouse continued to rise and in 1881 there were 329 inmates. A further loan of £2,000 was obtained in 1882 for the 'Erection of Infectious Hospital and Boundary Wall at Workhouse'. A comparison of the two ordnance survey maps of 1884 and 1904, reveals an extension to the rear of the small building at the north eastern end of the site with a wall enclosing it, and also two new buildings close by. It is probable that these three units were used for the isolation of inmates with infectious diseases. The high wall that surrounded the entire workhouse site appears to have been erected sometime between 1884 and 1904.

Plans were made to extend the workhouse further and in 1901, the board accepted a tender of £18,700, submitted by William Harvey Gibbs of King's Heath, for the erection of buildings designed by Cooper Whitwell and Sons, Architects of 23 Temple Row, Birmingham. Work was completed in March 1902. The guardians secured a loan of £23,000 for these extensions, and in 1904 a further loan for £2,000 to provide for the fixtures and fittings.

The builder was instructed to take down the 'cast iron coping and fence, brick wall and pier at the South end of the existing boundary wall of the West side of

A History of Selly Oak Hospital

The Isolation Block built in 1882 and added to in 1902. Later used for Maternity Services and then for Varicose Vein Clinics. (Valerie Arthur 2004)

A view down Raddlebarn Road with the infirmary in the distance. (Postcard courtesy Mary Harding)

present workhouse buildings' and to 'build a wall of Bromsgrove stone on either side of the Entrance with two curves of thirty foot radius'. Somewhat eroded, this wall still stands, flanking the West Gateway, which became the new entrance to the workhouse. Within the entrance archway was a foundation stone 'laid by Joseph Walter Esq., Chairman of the King's Norton Union House and Infirmary Committee in 1902'. Projecting backwards from the central building, two symmetrical wings housed clean clothing rooms, a disinfector and basement, receiving wards, a waiting room and the porter's office, living room and bedroom. White glazed bricks covered the whole height of the walls of the bathrooms, lavatories, scullery and pantry. The floors were laid with red paving tiles. Wrought iron balusters with cast iron finials were used for the stairs and landings, which were also paved with red tiles. American maple was laid on the floors of the receiving wards and waiting room.

M Block built in 1902. (Richard Daniels 2004)

Other buildings erected around that time were: a separate pavilion (M Block) for one hundred females; a smaller block for children (L Block); a general store and master's office; a sewing room and matron's office; a wood chopping, cutting and sawing workshop and a coal shed. At the north western corner of the site, on Oak Tree Lane and well away from the main workhouse buildings, another block was built for the casual poor.

After this massive project, little building activity appears to have been undertaken, apart from the erection of the master's house, later known as 'the old matron's house', and the laundry, which stood behind J Block. The green areas between M Block, the casual wards, the main workhouse buildings and the

*The Sewing Room built in 1902.
This was later the School of Nursing Number 2. (Richard Daniels 2004)*

perimeter walls, would have been used as airing yards and also for the cultivation of fruit and vegetables and to house pigs and chickens.

Nationally, from 1914-1919, the workhouse population began to drop, reducing the pressure on these institutions. Many were emptied and their inmates were transferred to neighbouring workhouses. At Selly Oak the workhouse became a hospital for the chronic sick; in 1948 it became a National Health Service hospital along with the adjourning infirmary. By that time, the corridors connecting E and J Blocks to K Block had disappeared, as had the walls between the airing yards that separated the various categories of inmates.

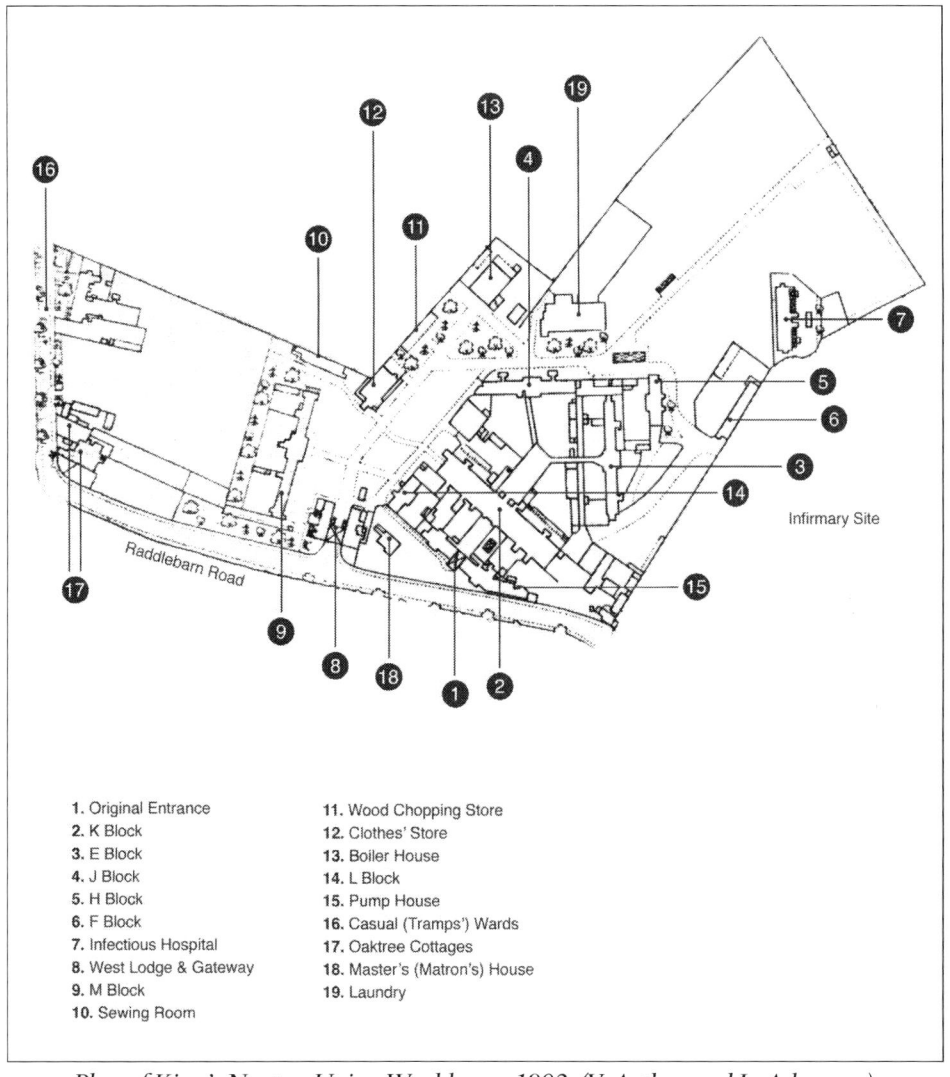

1. Original Entrance
2. K Block
3. E Block
4. J Block
5. H Block
6. F Block
7. Infectious Hospital
8. West Lodge & Gateway
9. M Block
10. Sewing Room
11. Wood Chopping Store
12. Clothes' Store
13. Boiler House
14. L Block
15. Pump House
16. Casual (Tramps') Wards
17. Oaktree Cottages
18. Master's (Matron's) House
19. Laundry

Plan of King's Norton Union Workhouse 1902. (V. Arthur and L. Adamson)

Chapter 3
―

Life in The Workhouse

Many contemporary reports from the early and mid-nineteenth century describe the inhumane conditions endured by workhouse inmates. The whole ethos of providing poor relief inside the workhouse was to ensure that life was so harsh that paupers would never want to return. Attitudes to the poor did, however, soften during the latter part of the nineteenth century as it became increasingly apparent that the majority of workhouse inmates were some of the most vulnerable people in society.

The two censuses of 1881 and 1901 provide details of the inmates of the King's Norton Union workhouse from which some comparisons can be drawn. The bald facts no doubt conceal pitiful stories of human misery and the reasons why these people arrived at the workhouse. A few records exist from the twentieth century and these help to build a picture of everyday life in the workhouse at that time. However, this limited information gives little evidence of how strictly the rules and regulations were implemented.

Workhouse Inmates in 1881
The census of 1881, shows that the workhouse at Selly Oak, like most workhouses nationally, was a repository for the old, the young and the ill. As shown in **Table 4**, there were 329 inmates, approximately a third of whom, (110), were children with ages ranging from 1 month to 16 years. Of these, 70 did not have any parents listed as being inmates of the workhouse so they were probably orphans or had been abandoned. There were 19 single parents with 40 children between them. Two of the single parents were men, one of whom is listed as being a widower. Only one of the mothers was married, the rest being unmarried, which in those days would have carried a dreadful social stigma for both the mother and the children. Not one of the child inmates is listed as having two parents. There was

only one small, complete family; a mother of 70, a father of 72 and an 'idiot' son of 46. There were 4 older married couples, (ages 53-91) and one young couple who were in their early twenties. There were 6 widows with ages ranging from 63-84 and 6 widowers whose ages ranged from 49-85. The census lists 19 idiots whose ages ranged between 13-78; 9 were male and 10 were female. The term 'idiot' was used widely and applied to the insane and those suffering from depression or epileptic fits. There were three blind inmates and one deaf and dumb man.

Workhouse Inmates 1901

Twenty years later, the census of 1901 gives a different picture. There were more inmates, the numbers having risen to 382. The greatest change was the increase in the number of inmates aged 60 years or more, half of whom were either widows or widowers. There was a significant decrease in the number of child inmates. By founding the Shenley Fields Cottage Homes in 1887, the guardians effectively removed children from the workhouse. There were far fewer single mothers: only three, each with one child.

Table 4

King's Norton Union Workhouse
Comparative Census Figures for 1881 and 1901
Status of Inmates

Year	Total number of Inmates	Children	Orphans/ abandoned	Inmates 60 years of age and over	Widow/ Widowers	Married Couples	Married	Unmarried	'Idiots' 'Imbeciles' Feeble minded Epileptics	Blind Deaf, Dumb Cripples
1881	329	110	70	99	13	5	30	171	19	4
1901	382	16	8	249	168	2	61	130	30	4

The term 'idiot' had been dropped and 'imbecile' or 'feeble minded' were used instead. There were 22 inmates listed in these two categories. Eight inmates suffered with epilepsy, a condition previously lumped under the term 'idiot'.

Workhouse Officers and Servants 1881

Table 5 lists the staff employed at the workhouse in 1881. Staff were generally very poorly paid and there was no career structure. The master of a workhouse, with between 500 to 600 inmates, would be lucky to earn £80 per annum, whilst a governor of a prison with 900 prisoners could earn as much as £600. How much was paid to staff at the King's Norton Union Workhouse is unknown.

Table 5
Workhouse Officers and Servants 1881

Resident (1881 Census)		Age years
Edward Williams	Master	31
Priscilla Williams	Matron	29
Henry Nuttall	Schoolmaster	24
Mary Nuttall	Schoolmistress	24
Caroline Weaver	Nurse	35
Jane Holter	Nurse	32
Joseph Shaw	Porter	43
Emily Shaw	Portress	34
George Crews	Shoemaker	23
Esther James	Cook	31
Non-Resident (Kelly's Directory of Birmingham 1881)		
F. Hollinshead	Surgeon	
Reverend T. Price	Chaplain	
William Morgan	Relieving Officer	

By 1902, the staff at the workhouse had increased, as shown in **Table 6**, as had the number of inmates.

Table 6
Officers and Servants at King's Norton Union Infirmary 1902
King's Norton Union Official Handbook 1902-1903

Officer	Name	Date of Appointment
Resident		
Master	Mr. E. J. Everdell	November 14th, 1900
Matron	Mrs. M. E. Morgan	December 31st, 1884
Asst. Matron	Miss Elizabeth Bailey	March 12th, 1890
Master's Clerk	Mr. H. A. Creaton	June 18th, 1902
Labour Master	Mr. B. Edworthy	May 2nd, 1888
Porter	Mr. C. E. Law	March 13th, 1901
Portress	Mrs. E. Law	March 13th, 1901
Attendant	Mr. T. E. Bant	July 9th, 1902
Do.	Mr. R. Harrington	March 28th, 1900
Do.	Mrs. S. Harrington	March 28th, 1900
Nurse	Miss Blanche Babb	February 6th, 1895
Assistant Nurse	Miss Alice Weaver	September 12th, 1901
Nurse	Miss E. Mullett	March 12th, 1890
Laundress	Mrs. Ada Edmunds	December 23rd, 1900
Children's Attendant	Miss L. Edworthy	December 7th, 1898
Non-Resident		
Chaplain	Rev. Clement Sharpe	January 10th, 1900
Visiting Medical Officer	Mr. Francis Hollinshead M. D.	March 15th, 1871
Medical Officer	Mr. Julian Hora	July 12th, 1899
Cook	Mr. R. Eite	September 29th, 1900
Engineer	Mr. Henry Smith	November 19th, 1884
Baker	Mr. James Ward	November 4th, 1891
Assistant Baker	Mr. F. Canning	April 8th, 1902
Carpenter	Mr. Edwin Boraston	April 4th, 1883
Bricklayer	Mr. James Quinn	July, 1882
Shoemaker	Mr. A. Bennett	September 29th, 1900

The Workhouse Master

Mr. E.J. Everdell was the workhouse master in 1902. Rules and regulations from the Poor Law Commission in London set out that workhouse masters had to be at least 21 years old, preferably with a spouse, who would normally take on the role of workhouse matron. They also had to be able to keep accounts, to know their place, to be respectful of the guardians, tolerant yet firm with the other workhouse officers and inmates, and also able to control their own behaviour, temper and language and that of others. In addition they had a duty to ensure that not only were inmates clothed, fed and cared for physically and spiritually but that they were industrious, orderly, punctual and clean.

Mr. Creaton was the master's clerk; his duties were to record the number of inmates, to keep an inventory of the property and clothes of the deceased and to estimate the quantities of provisions that were required and used.

The Matron

The matron, Mrs. M. E. Morgan, was the widow of the previous master and had served since 1884. Her job was to act as a deputy for the master, supervise the female inmates, take responsibility for the domestic management of the workhouse and for the care of nursing mothers and the sick.

The Porter and Portress

The porter and portress, Mr. and Mrs. Law had many duties, but their principal responsibility was to ensure that the workhouse was kept secure and to enforce obedience from the inmates.

They took charge of the gate and of the workhouse keys, admitting paupers and visitors, and locking up at night. They also kept records of any persons visiting the workhouse and details of their business.

The Nurses and Attendants

There were two nurses, one assistant nurse and three attendants; two male and one female and one children's attendant. Their duties were to assist the master and matron in the care of sick paupers, nursing mothers and children.

Non-Resident Staff
The Medical Officers

Mr. Julian Hora, the medical officer, was appointed in 1899. The visiting medical officer, Mr. Francis Hollinshead, had been appointed to the post in 1871. They examined all paupers on admission and gave directions for their welfare, diet and care, and vaccinated any children who had not already been treated. If the master called for them, they were expected to be punctual in attending to any inmates. They recorded all deaths and it was also their responsibility to report any defects in the drainage, ventilation or warmth of the workhouse.

The Chaplain

The Reverend Clement Sharpe was the chaplain whose duty it was to assess and attend to the moral and religious state of the inmates, teach children who belonged to the Church of England and visit sick paupers to offer religious consolation. He also had to preach a sermon to the workhouse inmates every Sunday, Good Friday and Christmas Day.

Admission to the Workhouse

West Lodge built in 1902. Paupers were admitted into the workhouse through these doors. (Richard Daniels 2004)

It is not too difficult to imagine the misery of those denied outdoor relief and who were subsequently admitted into the workhouse. The rules and regulations show how the inhumanity of the system immediately swung into operation. On admission all paupers were searched, the males by the porter and the females by the matron.

Any alcohol or tobacco was confiscated as the authorities were fearful of drunkenness, insubordination and fire. Families were split up and individuals placed in separate receiving wards. Communication with the opposite sex was forbidden. From then on husbands, wives and children had little or no chance of even catching a glimpse of each other. The new block to the west of the site (M Block) was specifically for women. In the other blocks, separate entrances, corridors and staircases to the individual wards ensured there was no contact between male and female inmates. Even the airing yards were segregated and surrounded by high walls.

After a medical examination, new inmates were assigned to the ward for their designated class.

Table 7

Classes of inmates in the workhouse

Males	Females	Children
Class 1 Aged or infirm	Class 4 Aged and infirm	Class 7 Under 7 years
Class 2 Able-bodied over 15 years	Class 5 Able-bodied over 15 years	
Class 3 Boys 7-15 years	Class 6 Girls 7-15 years	

Before going to their specific ward, paupers were thoroughly cleansed and given workhouse clothes. Their own clothes were disinfected, cleaned, labelled with their name and stored. On discharge their clothes were given back to them. The clothes of those who died in the workhouse were disposed of according to the guardians' wishes, which usually meant that they were sold. Men were given coats, jackets, waistcoats, trousers, shirts, shoes, stockings, hats, and handkerchiefs. Women received gowns, petticoats, shifts, aprons, handkerchiefs, shoes, stockings, caps and bonnets. Garments which would have been worn by previous inmates, were shapeless, and badly made in poor quality material, often with a pattern of broad vertical stripes, numbered and marked with the name of the union.

The Daily Routine followed the rules set out by the Poor Law Commissioners

5.00 a.m.	Rising bell, roll call and inspection of inmates.
6.00 a.m. – 7.00 a.m.	Prayers read by the Master and breakfast. Inspection of the sleeping wards by the Master and Matron.
7.00 a.m. – 12 noon	Work
12 noon – 1.00 p.m.	Dinner
1.00 p.m. – 6.00 p.m.	Work
6.00 p.m. – 7.00 p.m.	Prayers read by the Master
7.00 p.m. – 8.00 p.m.	Supper
8.00 p.m.	Bed

During the day, able-bodied males worked under the supervision of the labour master; chopping wood, breaking stones, attending to the pigs, working in the vegetable gardens and grounds, or in the bakery. This labour brought in a profit for the guardians and also supplied food for the workhouse. Other inmates helped maintain the buildings by assisting the engineer, bricklayer and carpenter and others cleaned the male wards or attended to male inmates. Able-bodied women kept the female wards and corridors clean, attended to female inmates, laundered linen, stockings and clothes, and assisted the cook.

The master and matron inspected the sleeping wards before 9 pm in the winter and 10pm in the summer, to check that the inmates were in bed and that all fires and lights were put out. The wards would have been poorly furnished with iron bedsteads and straw mattresses, long forms, stools and tables and a central stove to provide some heat.

Workhouse Food

The amount and type of food that inmates were given were set out by the Poor Law Commissioners on a three day rota, and depended upon the classification of each inmate. Detailed records were kept of the amounts and the weights of all portions and of any food that was not eaten. Breakfast and supper might be bread or gruel, cheese or dripping, milk, tea, sugar, and butter. Lunch was only provided for some classes, possibly the children, and consisted of seed cake or bread and dripping. At dinner bread, soup, potato hash, meat, potatoes, rice pudding, and occasionally vegetables were served. **Table 8** sets out the breakfast rota for one day. It is interesting to note that vagrants did not receive any breakfast.

Table 8
Breakfast Record for 2nd October 1900 for 312 inmates

N.B. There are more than 7 inmate classes and the amounts for classes 8, 8a, 9 and 9a suggest these are infants (Daily Provisions consumption account 1900-1901 GB/KN/21/1 Birmingham Central Library)

Class	Number	Absent	Sick	Bread	Gruel	Tea	Butter	Milk
1	17		4	7oz @	1.5 pint @			
-	13					1pt	half oz	
2	135		7			ditto	ditto	
3	2			Ditto	Ditto			
4								half pint
4a	5		1					ditto
5	26		5	6oz	1.5			
-	16			ditto		1pt	ditto	
6	83		38	ditto		ditto	ditto	
7	-			5oz	1.5 pint			
8	2			4oz	half pint			
8a	3			3oz	ditto			
9	6			2oz	ditto			
9a	4			1oz	ditto			
Vagrants								

In the early days of the poor law, the commissioners had forbidden any extras, even if they were funded by private charity. But by 1847, guardians were authorised to provide Christmas extras out of the rates. On Christmas Day in 1902, at King's Norton Union Workhouse the record for provisions was more substantial and varied considerably from the normal daily rations. There were 280 pounds of bread, 10 ounces of tea, 311 pounds of sugar, 224 pounds of butter, eggs 142, currants 270 pounds, flour 100 pounds, meat 532 pounds, suet 188 pounds, potatoes 400 pounds, milk 95 pints, raisins 222 pounds and coffee 20 pounds. The total daily ration of meat for the workhouse was normally 70 pounds.

In 1896, following a report from a Royal Commission on the aged poor, guardians were ordered to discriminate between respectable, aged paupers and those who were poor due to their own misconduct. Wards for the aged, who had previously led moral and respectable lives, were often called 'Merit' wards to distinguish them from the wards for rowdier paupers from rougher backgrounds. In 1893, changes in the rules allowed old people to be provided with dry tea, milk and sugar so they could brew their own tea.

King's Norton Union. (Merit Ward)
On the back of this postcard is written 'They would put you in this ward if you would behave yourself.' (Postcard courtesy of Mary Harding)

By the turn of the century more concessions were being urged on the poor law unions, such as allowing old people, aged over 65 years, to get up and go to bed when they liked, and providing them with locked cupboards for their possessions. Slowly changes were implemented and rooms were provided for older married couples, day rooms were open to both sexes and, in some unions, workhouse uniform disappeared. It was also suggested that all but the most untrustworthy old people should be allowed to go out of the workhouse for walks. By then the aged poor were often better off than their counterparts outside the workhouse walls.

The Sick in the Workhouse

By the mid-nineteenth century there were fewer able-bodied inmates in the workhouse and many more sick and infirm for whom no provision had been made under the New Poor Law of 1834. Many of the sick suffered appalling conditions and treatment. Facilities for washing and hygiene were sparse and inmates lay on thin, flock filled mattresses on beds constructed from iron bars, without pillows and with few blankets or coverings. There were no chairs for those who could get out of bed and it was not uncommon for the sick to spend years on the same ward without ever getting out of bed. Poor law nurses were few and usually old. They were expected to work for no pay, to sleep on the wards and to eat the same food as the inmates. Often the task of caring was given to fellow paupers who were given no guidance on how to look after the sick, and were often rewarded for their labours with an allowance of beer or gin. It was common knowledge that many nurses neglected their charges and were not averse to demanding bribes from defenceless patients.

Matters came to a head in London, during the 1860s, where many workhouses already had separate infirmaries. Public awareness of the plight of the sick in workhouses was raised with the description in The Times on Christmas Eve 1864 of the suffering of a 'well made and muscular man aged 28 years', who died in the Holborn Workhouse from 'untreated sores'. Then in 1865, The Lancet publicised weekly results from its independent 'Sanitary Commission for investigating the State of Infirmaries and Workhouses'. This enquiry highlighted that six of the infirmaries investigated in thirty-two London metropolitan workhouses, 'were entirely improper residences for the sick let alone the able-bodied'. The Commission reported that paid, trained nurses were few and that nursing care varied from that provided by efficient staff to that provided, or not, by unsupervised, decrepit paupers. It also reported that there were too few medical officers, the wards were small, and that a lack of sanitation and ventilation produced an unhealthy and filthy environment.

In response to this publicity the Poor Law Board sent a letter to all guardians in 1866 discouraging the use of paupers as assistant nurses, and suggesting that a sufficient number of paid nurses should be employed. Matters did improve in London but were short-lived and nearly thirty years later, in 1894, a 'Report on the Nursing and Administration of Provincial Workhouses and Infirmaries', commissioned by The British Medical Journal, found conditions similar to those that were published in The Lancet three decades previously. In 1897, the Local Government Board banned all pauper nurses. Despite this many continued to be employed as 'helpers'.

As early as 1865, Agnes Jones, a Nightingale nurse, who was matron of the Liverpool Workhouse Infirmary with the care of 1,300 patients and 60 nurses, stated that respectable women could only be attracted to nursing in the workhouse if they were properly paid and provided with decent food and accommodation. In 1860 a nurse's salary was £8-£10 a year and ten years later this had risen to £20-£30 for a trained nurse, £50 for a ward sister and £100 for a matron. Eventually as pay and conditions improved, more trained nurses were recruited to workhouse infirmaries and by 1897, when the workhouse infirmary opened at Selly Oak probationer nurses were employed and trained there.

Evidence of poor care at King's Norton Union Workhouse 1901
At the King's Norton Union workhouse there is evidence of the poor nursing care received by one inmate, who unfortunately was not nursed in the infirmary. On 8th March 1901, James Timmins wrote to the Local Government Board in Whitehall complaining about his treatment. He had suffered for nine years from paralysis caused by lead poisoning, a condition associated with his occupation as a house painter. Lead was used in both interior and exterior house paint until it was banned in 1978. Mr. Timmins was a twenty-nine year old batchelor from Witney in Oxfordshire. In his letter, he described how he was 'attended by a certified imbecile and an epileptic inmate'. He was dropped by one such 'carer' and suffered a fractured tibia which healed, but then he was dropped again and hurt his spine severely. He describes Block III (*which block this was is unknown*) as being used for 'convalescents, epileptics, feeble old men and helpless cases which are thrown together promiscuously'. Apparently, the certified inmate was 'rough and wild', worked from early in the morning until late at night and was not available when needed. A following letter from the guardians stated that Mr. Timmins had been supplied with a wheeled carriage within three days of his letter and that he was now content and sorry that he had written to the authorities. Perhaps this helpless man had little choice but to feel content.

This sort of treatment would explain why, even in the late 20th century, older patients had a groundless fear of admission to the geriatric wards at Selly Oak Hospital. For them the workhouse connotations were within living memory.

Chapter 4

The Casual (Vagrants') Wards

Travelling or 'tramping' was a way of life for many people during the nineteenth and early twentieth century. Some 'professionals' often took their families with them and tramped from one workhouse to another seeking employment along the way. These travelling folk were known as 'tramps', 'vagrants', 'wayfarers', 'casuals' or the 'casual poor'. They were regarded with distrust by the general public who considered them to be a nuisance and they were, in the main, treated harshly by workhouse officials and the police.

Tramping was a seasonal way of life and as summer approached there was a trend to move away from the towns and cities into the country from indoor to outdoor jobs. In the towns, smithies and factories were often closed as trade slackened off and this offered a chance to escape from factory hazards, such as foul air and unguarded, dangerous machinery.

During August and September, many country fairs were held which attracted hawkers hoping to sell their wares and labourers looking for local seasonal employment. In the Midlands, tramps and their families descended on rural areas such as the Vale of Evesham for fruit picking, or Herefordshire for the hop picking. A useful income could be earned when the whole family worked alongside each other.

When winter set in, there was a drift back to the towns as manufacturing picked up ready for Christmas. General labourers, who might be found navvying on the canals and railways during the summer, took their skills into the gas works as the demand for light and heat increased with the shorter, colder, winter days. Many found employment on public building projects in the expanding cities, working on town halls, schools, libraries, municipal baths and churches. Big contract jobs usually continued despite the bad weather as did the building of private housing and the laying of drains and sewers. Work was also to be found in other trades such as brickmaking and in the breweries where production increased after the hop harvest.

Many tramps slept 'rough' in summer under hedges or haystacks and in winter close to brick or gas works, factories and under bridges where some warmth and shelter could be found. Those with some money, usually obtained by begging or hawking, could find cheap basic accommodation in the numerous lodging houses of most towns and cities, and free accommodation in refuges set up by charitable organisations such as the Salvation Army. Workhouses, which were conveniently placed within a day's tramp from each other, were another option, where in exchange for some form of labour on the following day, a night's accommodation and food could be secured.

The Poor Law Act of 1834 made no mention of tramps and therefore initially no provision was made for them. Their existence was largely denied by the authorities, even though large numbers of paupers were tramping the roads, often miles from their native parishes and therefore not eligible for local poor relief. Vagrancy was not considered to be a matter for the poor law unions but one to be dealt with by the police. Stories of tramps being turned away from union workhouses and subsequently dying from starvation and exposure shocked the general public. In 1837 the poor law commissioners recommended that these 'wayfarers' be given a meal and shelter in return for undertaking a 'task'. The commissioners also recommended that casual wards should be separate from the workhouse and that conditions in these should be harsher than those for ordinary workhouse inmates. The Pauper Inmates Discharge and Regulation Act of 1871, tightened up the rules around performing a task, stating that casuals were not allowed to leave until at least 11am on the day after their arrival, and then only after completing a task. In 1882, further legislation meant that those admitted to the casual wards had to do one full day's work, leaving at 9am on the third day after arrival on the first visit in the month, and two days' work, staying until the fourth day on the second visit within the month. These severe restrictions worked against those genuinely seeking employment and to rectify this poor law unions were advised in 1885, but not ordered, to allow paupers who had finished their task the night before to leave early at 5.30am in the summer and 6am in the winter. This condition was further extended in 1892 to anyone claiming to be genuinely wanting to work.

The general assumption was that the majority of tramps were ne'er do wells who were not interested in working but preferred to beg. Although many using the casual wards were beggars or petty tricksters there was some acknowledgment that a minority of those tramping the roads were decent people. The conditions in the casual wards were as one observer put it 'a disgrace to a civilised country

… the lowest of mankind deserve better treatment than that accorded to pigs, dogs and other animals of creation'. Such appalling conditions meant that many tramps used the casual wards as a matter of necessity rather than of choice. As one tramp remarked, 'whatever luck I had good or bad, I always managed to escape the workhouse: and was determined to walk all night, if needs be, rather than seek refuge in one of those places'.

Mary Higgs, Secretary of the Ladies Committee of Oldham Workhouse, was one of a few intrepid souls who disguised themselves as tramps, in order to find out exactly what conditions were like in the casual wards. In 1904 and 1906, accompanied by a female friend, she spent several nights in north country workhouses and was horrified to find them 'whether clinically clean or vermin-ridden, being uniformly cheerless and prison-like and the food even worse: saltless, or appallingly over-salted, gruel, dry bread and cheese, with no water allowed except at meal-times'. She discovered that 'everything seemed to be done to degrade women vagrants who were given no facilities to dry damp clothes and were strictly forbidden – even if put to work in the laundry – to wash their own garments'. Women also ran the risk of being solicited by male workhouse officials who expected sexual favours in return for extra rations.

Nationally there was no concerted approach to the treatment of the casual poor. Some unions exercised a softer policy than others which, it was believed, encouraged vagrancy and thus increased the problem for neighbouring unions. In 1904, admissions to casual wards reached an all time high and a government committee of enquiry, set up to investigate the problem, achieved nothing except to confirm that between a third and two thirds of those tramping the roads could be resettled into a normal life. Nothing was done to ensure this and tramps were treated even more severely as numbers continued to rise. In 1912, Vagrancy Committees were appointed in twenty different counties. Locally, food stations were set up on roads used by tramps in Warwickshire, Worcestershire and Staffordshire where 'four ounces of bread and two ounces of cheese (one and a half for women and children)' could be procured for their midday meal in exchange for a ticket issued on discharge from the workhouse that morning. By the beginning of the First World War, there were far fewer tramps as changes in the economy brought about an increase in regular employment, especially for the unskilled.

Opportunities for hawking goods around the countryside, a common occupation for many tramps, decreased as more and more shops were set up throughout rural England. Many casual wards were closed during the First World War and the introduction of hostels by philanthropic groups helped to ease the situation for tramps and vagrants in the big cities.

As the twentieth century progressed, the general attitude to tramps and vagrants began to soften with the realisation that many were either lunatics or too old or too ill to work. Treatment became more lenient and in the remaining casual wards conditions slowly improved. Instead of hammocks there were mattresses and iron bedsteads, clean nightshirts were given to new arrivals, and showers were installed in some places to ensure that tramps bathed in clean water. Facilities for washing underclothes and making tea were often provided. The number of tramps seeking admission to casual wards decreased, until the economic depression of the early 1920s, when casual wards were enlarged to accommodate the greater number of people tramping from one end of the country to the other in search of work. In 1930, Public Assistance Committees took over the work of the Poor Law Unions and reorganised local facilities by closing some casual wards and expanding others.

In 1912, when the King's Norton Union poor law responsibilities were transferred from the county of Worcestershire to the city of Birmingham the workhouse on Raddlebarn Road was renamed the Birmingham Union Workhouse. In 1913, the guardians decided to close the tramp wards at Selly Oak and Erdington (Aston Union) and tramps were accommodated in the casual wards at Western Road House (Dudley Road Hospital). When this move took place is uncertain for the casual wards of the Birmingham Union at Oak Tree Lane were still listed in Kelly's Directory of 1916.

One memory remained for a lady who described her two aunts' house next to the casual wards on Oaktree Lane '*my mother said that the window that faces their front door is where the tramps used to queue at night. I don't know whether it was for food or accommodation. The front door had bars because they were afraid of the vagrants. That's what my mother told me – it was the tramps' ward*'.

The Casual Wards at King's Norton Union Workhouse at the beginning of the 20th Century

The new casual wards were built in 1901 facing onto Oak Tree Lane at a distance from the main workhouse and are easily identified on the ordnance survey map of 1904. At that time the tramp master was Mr. W. Broadley. He was appointed in May 1888, and his wife Mrs. M.M.H. Broadley, who was appointed in December 1900, was the tramp mistress.

The casual wards had two entrance doors at the front, which indicates that men and women were admitted separately. On the ground floor there were individual cells and what was almost certainly a dormitory in the single storey extension on the right. Women and children would have been accommodated on the first floor, as was common practice. Generally women with children were lodged in a single

The Casual Wards, Oak Tree Lane. (Ruth Clarke 2013)

cell where they performed an allotted task which was often oakum picking. Arrangements for sleeping were makeshift; sometimes hammocks were slung up in the cells, whilst in the dormitories thin, straw mattresses were put on sleeping platforms divided into single areas by high wooden partitions. Within the building there would have been accommodation for the tramp master and his family and at least one bathroom, a disinfector for tramps' clothing, and a store.

Records show that the majority of tramps admitted to the casual wards at King's Norton Union during the six months from February to September 1901 were men. Admissions to the casual wards were usually higher in January and February as nearly all trades slumped after the festive period and work was more difficult to get. In the first week of February, one hundred and ninety men were admitted; their average age was forty-four years from a range of seventeen to seventy-eight years. The majority, one hundred and twenty-seven, gave their occupation as labourers but there were also skilled and semi-skilled workers. In September of that year ninety-nine men, sixty-six of whom were labourers, were admitted reflecting the seasonal decrease of vagrants in the towns when harvesting work was to be had in the countryside. The 'calling or occupation', of those admitted shows that England was indeed, in 1901, 'the workshop of the world'. It is interesting to note the diversity of occupations from those associated with the countryside such as corn miller, cowman and field worker, and trades associated with horses and horse transport: currier (groom), wheelwright, bridlemaker, saddlemaker, harness maker, drayman, coach maker and whipmaker, and those specifically associated with Birmingham and the Black Country such as metal bashing and the manufacturing trades.

During the same period a few tramps were absolved from doing a task for reasons of ill health. The oldest was a seventy eight year old hawker who was paralysed and the youngest a thirty year old with a broken hand. Only one man, a thirty year old bricklayer, was permitted to go without performing a task because he 'stated he had work to go to'. Although a sixty six year old sea captain was given the task of oakum picking, there is scant evidence of many traditional tasks such as this being undertaken to any extent. Oakum picking involved unravelling a set weight of small lengths of rope, an extremely arduous job, which caused the hands and fingers to blister and bleed. The oakum was sold to be mixed with tar for caulking wooden boats. Oakum picking is listed in the expenditure records as a receipt, but it appears to be in decline; no sums of money were received for this in the years 1903-1906. However, this task did depend upon there being a supply of oakum and it may have been unavailable. Another traditional task, stone breaking, is shown as bringing an income of £9 in 1904, increasing to £19 in 1905 and decreasing again to £7 in 1906. Broken stone was sold for road making. Men given this task were usually confined in a cell or outbuilding where they were confronted with piles of granite, which they had to break into pieces small enough to go through a certain sized sieve. They did this by pounding the granite with a long, heavy metal bar for hours on end. Such unremitting, hard labour brought on severe pain in the back, shoulders, arms, wrists and hands besides making the hands blister and bleed. Only when they had completed this job were they released. Sawing wood for firewood seems to be a regular task for tramps with an income that rose from £152 in 1903 to £243 in 1906. Some vagrants were given the task of tending the gardens at 'The Oaklands', a large house on the corner of Oak Tree Lane and Raddlebarn Road, which had been purchased by the guardians in 1898, for use as a nurses' home.

To prevent tramps escaping without performing their set task, work-yards were usually surrounded by high walls surmounted by vicious iron spikes, hence 'The Spike' a nick name commonly used for the casual wards. The Selly Oak site was surrounded by high walls and some local residents recalled that the railings were removed during the Second World War for making armaments. Despite the high walls and spikes, six vagrants managed to 'escape' during the six months of February to September in 1901, one over an iron gate, two while going to the workhouse, whilst three 'absconded'. Only one of these appears to have been caught; he was arrested and 'awarded seven days'. The police were often involved and one tramp is recorded as being arrested for refusing to work. Another, a twenty eight year old labourer, was also arrested for tearing up clothes and punished with twenty one days' hard labour. Tramps often tore up bedding, such as it was, not just to get replacements but to draw attention to the dreadful conditions in the casual wards. It was not uncommon for vagrants to break windows in the workhouse just so they could be handed over to the police and sent to gaol, where the food was better, work not so demanding and generally the conditions an improvement on those endured in the casual wards.

Most vagrants, admitted to the casual wards at King's Norton Union had slept only a few miles away on the previous night at places such as: Aston, Balsall Heath, Cradley and Redditch. However, a few are recorded as having travelled from further afield; Burton, Gloucester, Ledbury, Richmond, Stafford and London. To travel so far in only a day suggests that, unless they had slept rough, they arrived by means other than walking. Selly Oak was well served for transport with the major trunk road going south from Birmingham to Droitwich and the South West, as well as the railway and canal systems. Hitching a ride from a drayman, coachman or bargee would have been possible, as would be taking a tram or train ride if they had the fare.

Generally, tramps were regarded as a bad lot and their arrival at the workhouse was dreaded by officials and inmates alike as they were often drunk, noisy and destructive. All tramps were searched and some hid their valuables, sometimes burying them, before applying to the workhouse owing to the fact that they could be turned away if they had some money. They also ran the risk of their valuables being confiscated by union officials, or stolen from them by other tramps.

In 1901, at Selly Oak, twelve tramps, three of them women, were recorded as being in possession of money: one had a half penny, and six had one penny each. Other amounts found on individuals varied from two pennies up to the largest amount of three shillings and eleven pence, which was in the possession of a labourer. Any alcohol and tobacco was removed from them yet, despite such searches, many tramps smoked illicitly having smuggled tobacco into the wards. There are contemporary records of the appalling behaviour of tramps in the casual wards, which other inmates had to endure through the long hours of the night when they were locked in together. Tramps communicated by scribbling on workhouse walls or by word of mouth. One policeman reckoned that it only took three days for details of extra searches and conditions at particular workhouses to circulate. Many would give false names to beat the system, since if they returned to the casual ward for a second time within the month they had to remain for four days which meant three days of labour.

Although whole families often took to the road there were far fewer women than men on the tramp after 1880, when it became compulsory for children to attend school until the age of thirteen. During the school holidays, which coincided with the sowing and harvest of crops, women with school age children took to the roads with their menfolk. Potato picking in particular was a popular but back breaking task for women and children.

Far fewer female than male tramps were recorded in 1901. In February, eleven women and five children were admitted, whilst in September twelve women but no children were given shelter. The main female occupation given was that of charwoman although some had more specific occupations, such as a housekeeper, button maker, seamstress, weaver, glove maker, spoon polisher, tailoress, thimble maker, factory hand and servant. A hawker and a street singer were possibly beggars. Women were allotted domestic duties such as scrubbing, cleaning, washing, and cleaning brasses. Some were absolved from tasks and allowed to leave without working, often because they were accompanied by children or were too ill or too feeble. Others were admitted to the workhouse on doctor's orders as 'being ill'. One reason given for not working was having a 'gathered' (septic) hand. A forty year old street singer with heart disease was given a cleaning job until 11 am. There were two records of women being the worse for drink: a thirty nine year old laundress with a four year old boy and a charwoman of sixty five. One thirty year old charwoman, was found to have nine pennies when searched. She had five children: a girl of twelve years, three boys of ten, five and two years respectively and a baby daughter of nine months. It is recorded that she 'took a tram from Birmingham for a night's lodging at this casual ward'.

Tramps were discharged from the casual ward on the second day after their admission having completed a task. At Selly Oak in 1901, one sixty-one year old iron worker 'produced a letter for work at Spark Brook' and was allowed to leave without undertaking any labour. The Admissions and Discharge book lists the places that those who were discharged were going to; some travelled locally whilst others went to places at a greater distance such as Bristol, Burton, Cheltenham, Derby and Stafford. Many tramps worked a circuit and no doubt some of them eventually ended up back at the casual wards on Oak Tree Lane.

Chapter 5

King's Norton Union Workhouse Infirmary

As a result of the Poor Law Amendment Act of 1834 most workhouses made some provision for the care of sick paupers, usually in separate wards from the able-bodied inmates. The guardians had a responsibility to provide medical attention and in-patient facilities and this meant that there was some sort of hospital provision throughout the country. However, as the numbers of sick and infirm in workhouses increased, scandals emerged about the appalling neglect that many of them endured. The need for better care, especially nursing care, was taken up by reformers keen to change the Poor Law and public opinion was awakened to the fact that the majority of inmates were elderly and often chronically sick or mentally ill.

The Metropolitan Poor Act of 1867 enabled the guardians of the London unions, where the problem of sick paupers was particularly acute, to set up infirmaries separate from the workhouses. It was at least another two or three decades before the sick poor were removed from provincial workhouses to separate workhouse infirmaries. The same act also made provision for infectious diseases hospitals. But it was not until 1913 that the Mental Deficiency Act, which defined the various types of mental handicap, finally brought recognition of the needs of the mentally ill. Previously all types of sick paupers had been lumped together often with the mentally ill taking care of the chronic sick.

The Opening of the Infirmary 1897
There was already a small infirmary at the King's Norton Union Workhouse and also a separate infectious diseases block, but as the number of sick paupers increased this provision became inadequate. In 1893 the guardians took out a loan of £5,300 to purchase land adjacent to the workhouse for a new infirmary. Four guardians were appointed to visit other institutions in England and Scotland to

learn about the latest appliances, fittings, and machinery. Plans were drawn up and in 1894 a competition was held to find a suitable design. This was won by Daniel Arkell for his 'Practical Design'. Three years later, in 1897 the King's Norton Union Workhouse Infirmary was opened. The New General Hospital in Steelhouse Lane (now the Birmingham Children's Hospital) was opened a few weeks before by Princess Christian, a daughter of Queen Victoria. This event had been marked by much celebration, whilst the opening of the infirmary at Selly Oak went largely unnoticed, perhaps because the one was financed by public subscription and the other was merely a workhouse establishment.

King's Norton Union Workhouse Infirmary circa 1900.
(copy of postcard courtesy of Medical Illustration – University Hospitals Birmingham NHS Foundation Trust)

Stifled Discussion, Furtive Mismanagement and Scandalous Waste
The original tender for building the infirmary was £18,000, but the Local Government Board recommended additions and improvements, which pushed the final cost up to £52,000. It was considered to be a very modern building and was a source of pride for some guardians, but one in particular, Lieutenant General Phelps, felt that it was an extravagant waste of rate-payers' money. He was so incensed that in 1900 he published a pamphlet dedicated to 'The Rate Payers of England and those of King's Norton in particular' with the title 'The Selly Oak Workhouse Infirmary; a strange tale of stifled discussion, furtive mismanagement and scandalous waste'. The pamphlet contained the report of a

public inquiry at which Lieutenant General Phelps gave evidence. He considered that the tender had been signed in haste, that the guardians had been unable to retract, and furthermore, the building had been 'ill designed and insufficiently discussed'. He drew attention to the fact it had been necessary to make alterations with the whole building being set back ten yards, changes were made to the dimensions of some of the rooms, and the drains were remodelled to conform

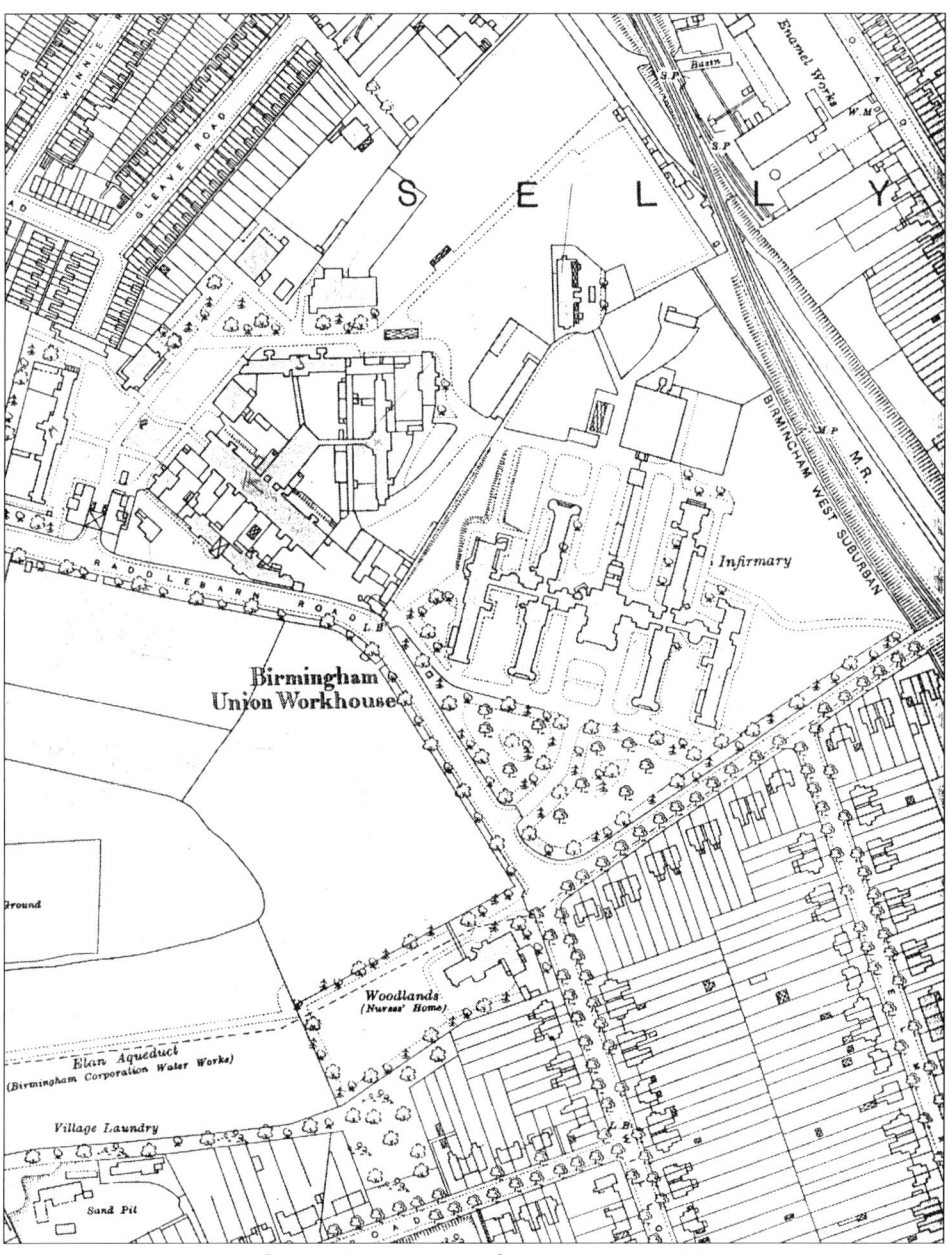

Ordnance Survey Map of King's Norton 1904.

with local bye-laws. Besides which, the water supply and the steam heating were overlooked and fresh contracts were entered into at extra expense. The coal shed was not large enough for the five tons of coal needed each winter that was brought by horse and cart from the nearby canal. The infirmary lacked a steward's office, a meat larder and a milk store. The kitchen roof was made of glass with the attendant risk of the staff being exposed to the risk of sunstroke 'in such summer weather as we have had'. There was insufficient residential accommodation for the medical and nursing staff and it had been necessary to buy houses in the neighbourhood to accommodate them. There was no operating theatre and no separate observation, locked, skin or epileptic wards. The lack of a mortuary meant that a temporary one was made in the infirmary dustbin, which was 'unseemly and led to premature burials'. In conclusion, Lieutenant General Phelps drew up rules 'to prevent a recurrence of the scandalous waste disclosed'. The Local Government Board public inquiry found that there was no case for Lieutenant General Phelps' allegations but it is not recorded whether the ratepayers agreed.

The infirmary was for the reception and treatment of sick paupers belonging to the union and was officially 'deemed to be a distinct establishment from the other workhouse of the union'. As can be seen from the ordnance survey map of 1904, a wall separated the establishments and each had its own entrance. The infirmary entrance was at the corner of Raddlebarn Road and had very impressive

King's Norton Union Workhouse Infirmary circa 1900.
There are only two ward blocks at this time. (Postcard courtesy of Mary Harding)

iron railings and gates, porters' lodge and drive, which led to the main central doorway.

The infirmary buildings were of 'red brick, relieved by dark-red coloured bricks and terracotta strings, the roofs being covered with bright red Broseley tiles' and the style being a 'free treatment of the Renaissance'. The original buildings were two pavilions (which became known as B and C Blocks) with eight Nightingale wards, each with a bathroom, sluice, side rooms and a balcony for convalescent patients. Small windows from the nurses' duty rooms and the ward kitchens looked into the ward. The fact that the labour wards were on C Block suggests that this whole block was for females. There were 250 beds and an isolation block. Plenty of space remained on the site for more buildings to be eventually erected.

Workhouse regulations of necessity influenced the design; the receiving wards of the male and female pavilions had 'no direct internal communication between them' in line with the rules that male and female paupers should be separated within the workhouse. Although the infirmary was considered to be up to date, the internal walls were not plastered; painted brick was economic and considered quite acceptable for sick paupers. More practically, use was made of natural light with large windows on either side of the wards. The floors were marble, mosaic a costly and chillier alternative to the original plan for wood block flooring.

The main central block, which separated the pavilions, contained doctors' rooms, a nurses' general sitting room, sewing rooms, matron's room, steward's

King's Norton Union Workhouse Infirmary circa 1908. There are now four ward blocks, note the main drive leading up to the central administration block. (Postcard courtesy of Mary Harding)

stores, a dispensary and a telephone exchange. Above this were rooms for nurses and female servants. A single storey kitchen and an administration block were built behind the central block and at the back of these were a boiler house, engine house, dynamo rooms, laundries and a water tower. Powerful steam engines created the electricity supply for lighting the whole of the infirmary and grounds. This was very modern as gas, rather than electricity, was used to light most buildings during the late nineteenth and early twentieth centuries.

The Infirmary at the beginning of the twentieth century
Nursing Staff

During the early years, the superintendent nurse, Miss Cowan, was under the jurisdiction of the workhouse master, but this changed in March 1900 when she was appointed matron of the infirmary. Miss Mina G. Cowan was thirty-five years old and well qualified for the post of matron, having trained for four years at the Royal Infirmary Glasgow, been a sister at the Royal Infirmary in Bristol and then head nurse at the Sunderland Union. In 1897 her salary was £60 per annum rising to £90 in 1904. Her main duties were to govern and control the nurses, female officers and servants of the infirmary and to see that the paupers were cleansed, clothed and placed in proper wards. She also had numerous housekeeping duties which involved superintending the making and mending of clothes, all properly marked with the words 'King's Norton Work House Infirmary', ensuring that all beds and bedding were kept clean and wholesome, receiving from the porter the keys of the infirmary gates and taking charge of all crockery, cooking and other utensils, clothing and linen. The assistant matron, Miss Eliza Butler, was forty-one years old and had been at the Sunderland Union with Miss Cowan. Her salary was £32 per annum. The nursing staff consisted of eight trained nurses and seventeen probationers, one of whom was fee-paying. Training took three years and probationers were accepted from 1897 when a medical officer was appointed, a stipulation made for training nurses under the Nursing in Workhouse Order of 1897.

The charge nurses (sisters) were trained and are recorded as being 'trustworthy', 'capable' and 'conscientious'. They were directly responsible for training the probationer nurses. The first probationers were paid £10 per annum. A few had previous nursing experience and most were aged over twenty-one, which was a regulation from the Local Government Board after 1900. They underwent a preliminary trial period of at least six weeks on the sick wards and after three years received their certificates of training, although some resigned because they were 'too delicate for training', 'unsuitable' or 'did not like the work'. The hours were very long, the work arduous and holidays were few. However, at that time, there were not many careers open to women and nursing provided an excellent opportunity for those who were intelligent, fit and not averse to hard work. Having completed three years of training and acquired a full certificate from their training school, nurses had the chance of independence and of a respected and responsible position in their own or another hospital.

The Steward

Management of the new infirmary was under the supervision of the steward, Thomas Skinner. He was thirty-two and had previously been assistant steward at the Metropolitan Asylums Board in Tottenham, London. His salary, in 1900, was £120 per annum with dinner and tea daily. He had to govern and control all male servants, receive all provisions and check them with the accounts besides keeping an estimate of the daily and weekly food consumption. A variety of food is listed in the records: bread, flour, beef, mutton, cheese, butter, eggs, tea, coffee, sugar lump, sugar moist, port, sherry, brandy, ale, porter, milk and fish. This list makes no mention of fruit or vegetables, which suggests that these may have been provided from the workhouse gardens. Medicines were few and a good diet, rich in protein and calories, was considered to be one way of getting patients restored to health. Port wine, ale, sherry and porter (beer) were commonly prescribed to help build up undernourished patients.

The steward's other duties were to keep a register of all births and deaths in the infirmary and a record of admissions and discharges. He was responsible for keeping accounts, an inventory of repairs and a record of clothing materials.

Medical Officers

The medical officer, at the infirmary and also at the workhouse, was Dr. Julian Hora. He was appointed in 1899 and lived in Selly Oak Cottages, Oak Tree Lane. His duties were to: 'Attend duly and punctually upon the paupers of the infirmary according to the necessities of their cases, and to give the requisite directions as to their treatment, nursing, diet and ventilation and conditions of the wards in which they are placed'. Diet, extras and medical treatment were entered on a card at the head of the patient's bed. Dr. Francis Hollinshead was the visiting medical officer for the workhouse and the infirmary. He attended the infirmary three days a week between the hours of eleven and one. The two doctors were responsible for all patients and also for the medical care of the workhouse inmates and the supervision of sixty-four imbecile beds. They dispensed medicines and attended difficult midwifery cases, which suggests that the nurses looked after most births. There is no record of Dr. Hora's and Dr. Hollinshead's salaries but these would have been an improvement on those received by earlier workhouse doctors, due to the efforts of the Poor Law Medical Officers' Association, which saw the salaries of Poor Law Union doctors rise from £50 per annum in the mid nineteenth century to as much as £350 per annum by the end of the century.

All paupers were admitted to the infirmary from the workhouse by a written order from the medical officer, unless there was a sudden emergency in which case they were admitted straight into the infirmary. It would appear that sick paupers in the infirmary fared somewhat better than those in the workhouse although they were subjected to the same demeaning admission procedures. Certainly the care given at the infirmary would have been as good as any in the country. The buildings were new, spacious, well ventilated and heated.

Nursing care was provided by an adequate number of probationers supervised by trained nurses and there was medical input from trained doctors. Rules and regulations from the poor law board were rigorous but ensured that patients received a wholesome diet and were provided with clean clothes and bedding. For most of the sick these conditions would have been much better than those in their own homes.

A report, published in 1909, by Dr. McVail to the Royal Commission on the Poor Law, found matters at the King's Norton Union Infirmary 'fairly satisfactory' but suggested that another resident doctor was needed. Dr. McVail did, however, approve of the infirmary and thought it 'was so handsome and well conducted that the patients did not show the abhorrence of indoor relief which was found in other unions'. However, he also felt that 'the discipline and cleanliness of the life, the need for regular bathing and the want of opportunity for drinking had a very useful deterrent influence on the undeserved poor'. It seems that the attitude still persisted that the poor were in their situation because of fecklessness rather than circumstances beyond their control.

Inmates and patients in the King's Norton Union Workhouse and Infirmary 1901

The census of 1901 gives a picture of the patients in the infirmary and also of the inmates in the workhouse. There were more workhouse inmates (381) than infirmary patients (201). In both institutions there were babies up to a year old. In the infirmary there were four new babies who would have been born in the infirmary under the care of the midwifery sister. They were aged from 35 minutes to 2 weeks and their mothers were listed as patients. In the workhouse the nine babies, whose ages ranged from one month to a year, had no parents listed as inmates. They and four young children aged between two and four years old, who were also in the workhouse, were probably orphans or had been abandoned. There were eight children up to the age of sixteen in the infirmary, five of whom were classed as imbeciles. In total there were nine imbeciles in the infirmary. The workhouse had ten inmates classed as imbeciles, thirteen as feebleminded and eight as epileptics. Eight inmates of the workhouse were recorded as having paralysis whilst there were no paralysed patients in the infirmary. It seems that the workhouse was probably the last resort for many of these people, who might well have spent the rest of their lives there. What is surprising is that the patients in the infirmary seem to differ little in age distribution from the inmates of the workhouse. In both institutions, most were aged over 60 years old, and given that the hospital lacked an operating theatre it can be supposed that the hospital was caring mainly for sick paupers with chronic conditions. How it was decided in which establishment the sick were cared for must have depended entirely upon the gravity of their condition.

Enlargement of the Infirmary and building of The Woodlands Nurses' Home 1908

In 1904 the guardians took out a further loan of £1,600 to pay for the building of a mortuary and a nurses' dining room. The infirmary doubled in size in 1908 with the completion of, what became known as A and D Blocks, and also an extension to the isolation block. In 1908 the emergency theatre was opened in what later became the Endoscopy Unit.

A nurses' home, The Woodlands, was built on the opposite side of Raddlebarn Road to accommodate the increased numbers of nurses, which by then numbered forty. Prior to this the sisters and some nurses were accommodated in the Oaklands, a large Victorian house, which stood in five acres, on the corner of Raddlebarn Road and Oaktree Lane and was purchased by the guardians in 1898, with a loan of £5,000. This building was the King's Norton Union Nurses' Home until 1912 when it became a probation home for children. It was, no doubt, one of the buildings, referred to in Lieutenant General Phelps' pamphlet of 1900 that was bought to make up for the lack of nurses' accommodation in the new infirmary. Many years later it was demolished and the modern building on the site now houses the West Midlands Rehabilitation Centre.

Selly Oak Infirmary 1911

In 1911 a boundary change meant that Selly Oak became part of the city of Birmingham. The King's Norton Union Workhouse Infirmary was renamed Selly Oak Infirmary and the King's Norton Union Workhouse eventually became known as Selly Oak House.

Although public attitudes were changing there was still a stigma associated with poverty, disease and infirmity. Dr. F.W. Ellis, who was appointed in 1909 as

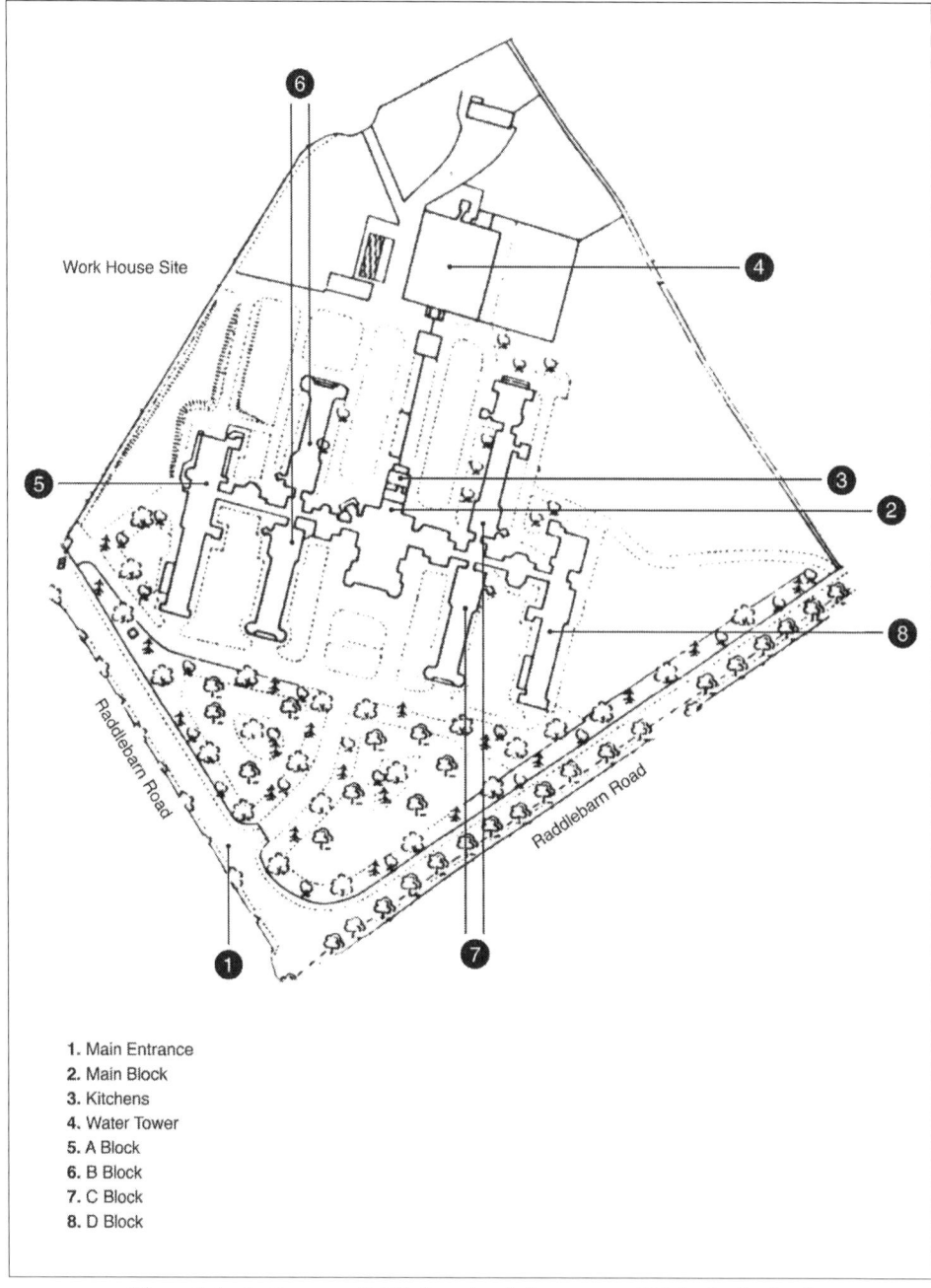

Plan of the Infirmary 1908. (Louise Adamson and Valerie Arthur)

medical officer at King's Norton Union Workhouse and Infirmary and later as chief medical officer to the new amalgamated Birmingham Union, certainly did not share the general opinion that the poor and diseased were ne'er-do-wells. In a report of 1912, this pioneering physician asked the question "Are old age and sickness sins? If not, why should the finger of scorn be pointed at these unfortunates?" Dr. Ellis had a great understanding of the plight of the poor and was determined to better their lot. He set about the task of classifying those in his care to improve their treatment and rehabilitation. There was ample scope for this in his position of responsibility for all medical care within the large Birmingham Union. In 1914 his classification scheme was approved by the guardians and adopted as a standard to be used within the various institutions of the union. The guardians endorsed the scheme, believing it was sound enough in theory to require no alteration in practice.

World War I 1914-1918
During the First World War, guardians of the Birmingham Union placed parts of their institutions at the disposal of the War Office. Thus Selly Oak Infirmary saw the arrival of patients displaced from Dudley Road Infirmary, which was taken over for use as a military hospital. Furthermore the guardians authorised the use of two separate wards at Selly Oak for the reception of air raid casualties.

Selly Oak Infirmary 1922-1930
In 1922, a third medical officer was appointed to cope with the increasing numbers of patients. At a hospital committee meeting in 1923, it was reported that the infirmary was overcrowded with more than 490 patients being treated in an institution built for 250 and, moreover, that the kitchens were insufficient to cater for these numbers.

There was still a lack of accommodation for the nursing staff whose numbers had steadily increased. In particular the number of probationer nurses being accepted for training had risen in the years after the First World War. Large numbers of probationer nurses were essential to care for patients most of whom suffered with chronic medical conditions, which required that they be nursed in bed for weeks and often months. In 1929 an extension to The Woodlands Nurses' Home was completed as was the medical residence built opposite the main door to the infirmary, which accommodated the increased number of seven full time doctors.

The first pathological, X-ray and physiotherapy services were introduced in 1923 in line with the new advances in the diagnosis and care of patients. The physiotherapy facilities were in a wooden hut formerly used as an army hut in Sutton Park during the First World War. A charted physiotherapist worked there on one or two afternoons per week. In the same year, a temporary out-patient department was set up in the former labour wards (C5 and C6) and was to remain there for the next forty years. Slowly the infirmary was becoming removed from its workhouse origins and especially so in 1925, when the ward walls were finally plastered; an improvement on the previous 'workhouse associated' painted brickwork.

Lieutenant General Phelps had noted in 1900 that the new infirmary lacked an operating theatre. This facility was long awaited, even though in 1923 an 'urgent need' for an operating theatre was highlighted. Despite a full time theatre sister being appointed at the same time, it seems that the emergency theatre, built in 1908, had to suffice for a few more years. A proposal that the old nurses' dining room should be adapted as a theatre was not taken up due to various delays. The number of surgical cases increased from 1,247 in 1924 to 2,259 in 1927. Action was needed and in 1928 it was suggested that 'an entirely new operation suite be erected at the east end of D Block'. This, however, would include only one theatre 'in order to reduce to a minimum the expenditure for the time being'. It was not until 1931, when the infirmary was no longer a workhouse institution, that there was an operation suite at the hospital.

Selly Oak Hospital 1930
In 1930 when the administrative structure of the Poor Law was finally dismantled, Selly Oak Infirmary became Selly Oak Hospital, one of the Birmingham Municipal Hospitals. The institution that Birmingham City Council took over was an impressive and well-run establishment due to the foresight and planning of Dr. Ellis. Recognising the increased demand to accommodate the chronic sick, the Board of Guardians had planned to erect a new block with 150 beds for these patients. In 1932, instead of a new block, Birmingham City Council approved a plan to remodel K Block at an estimated cost of £28,000. This, however, would have provided insufficient beds to meet the demand. The Ministry of Health refused Birmingham City Council permission to spend this amount and advised that K Block should be demolished. This did not happen and the chronic sick were cared for there until the block was taken over by the physiotherapy and occupational therapy departments in 1975. The overcrowding at Selly Oak Hospital was somewhat relieved when the Queen Elizabeth Hospital was opened in 1938. The City Council 'rented' 64 beds there for a couple of years to help with the situation. In 1934, the new biochemistry and pathology laboratories were opened. When the hospital laundries were closed in 1936 another association ended as many workhouse inmates had been employed there in the early days.

It seems that at some time during the 1930s the alphabetical labelling of the wards and blocks was introduced. No records remain of the early use for the individual wards, but a postcard from the 1930s shows some of them identified: Ward A1 (Babies), Ward B1 (Accident), Ward D5 (Maternity), and Ward C3 (Medical).

Appointment of a Lady Almoner

A lady almoner, the equivalent of today's hospital social workers, was appointed in December 1937. There were few such posts outside London. The first lady almoner ever appointed in England was at the Royal Free Hospital in 1895. Not until the implementation of the National Health Service did almoners became regular members of the hospital staff. Their role developed from the voluntary work of lady guardians who sat on workhouse visiting committees. Their prime concern then had been for the welfare of the women and young girls in the lying-in (maternity) wards of workhouses, many of whom carried the stigma of 'fallen women', in other words unmarried mothers. Concern for the aftercare of patients was integral to the role of the lady almoner, one aspect being the arrangement of care in convalescent homes so that recovering patients did not go back immediately to the poor living condition which had often brought about or exacerbated their conditions in the first place. Lady almoners were also responsible, primarily in the voluntary hospitals, for assessing whether patients were able to pay for some or all of their care.

In 1940, the medical superintendant of Selly Oak Hospital, Mr. R. Kelman, stated that there were no 'special paying beds' and 'that those who belong to the Hospitals' Contributory Scheme pay nothing. Then we have an almoner who decides what the others can afford'. At the time there was widespread concern that more affluent patients were taking advantage of the system and occupying hospital beds needed for poorer people.

World War II 1939-1945

Civilian victims of the many air raids over Birmingham, aimed at the factories providing arms and aircraft to support the war effort, were treated at Selly Oak Hospital. Wounded servicemen were taken to the Queen Elizabeth Hospital. Both establishments suffered from a shortage of medical staff as many doctors had joined up to serve at the Front. It is recorded that Mr. R.P.S. Kelman, the medical superintendent at Selly Oak Hospital, enlisted along with several hospital porters. When they returned it was to a changing world of the Welfare State and the National Health Service.

Part Two
1948-2012

Introduction

Since the introduction of the National Health Service advances in surgery and medicine have changed the concept of patient care. Previously the emphasis had been on long periods of bed rest and convalescence but this has altered over the ensuing years as the emphasis has shifted to rehabilitation. The introduction of sophisticated investigative procedures has resulted in early diagnosis, while new medicines and surgical operations help patients to recuperate more quickly and spend less time in hospital. This has inevitably changed the organisation and use of hospitals.

The National Health Service
In 1942 William Beveridge published a report commissioned by the government on how to rebuild Britain when the war ended. His recommendation was that the five 'Giant Evils' of 'Want, Disease, Ignorance, Squalor and Idleness' should be fought. In the General Election of 1945 the Labour Party defeated the Conservative Party, led by Winston Churchill, and the new Prime Minister, Clement Attlee, introduced the Welfare State, even though the Labour Party had initially rejected the concept as recommended by William Beveridge. The Welfare State was a system of benefits to provide for those in need and also to provide free medical treatment for all 'from cradle to grave'. The National Health Service (NHS) Act was passed in 1946 and implemented on July 5th 1948. From that day all medical treatment was free; those who previously would have been deterred from seeking treatment through lack of money would now be able to seek help.

The challenge to provide such a service in post war austerity Britain for many more patients was enormous.

Fourteen Regional Hospital Boards were established in England and Wales to oversee the provision of health care in their own areas. Each board appointed management committees to undertake responsibility for the numerous establishments that were now under their jurisdiction. These establishments cared for a wide range of people: the chronic and acute sick, the elderly, the young, the disabled and the mentally ill, often in old and poorly maintained buildings. The success of the new NHS depended not only upon sufficient numbers of medical and nursing staff, but also on administrators and planners who were willing to acknowledge the huge and varied changes that were taking place in medicine, and how best to use and adapt institutional buildings, many of which had been built originally as workhouses.

Over the ensuing years there were more and more changes. Nationally many residential homes and smaller hospitals were eventually decommissioned and the sites were redeveloped for housing. Some large general hospitals continued to provide a comprehensive service while they also became recognised as centres for certain specialities. This led to a huge programme of building, renovation work and reorganisation of health services during the following decades. This was to culminate in Birmingham with the opening in 2010 of the new Queen Elizabeth Hospital in Edgbaston, which was built to replace the Queen Elizabeth Hospital and Selly Oak Hospital. It was the first acute hospital to be built in Birmingham since 1938, when the first Queen Elizabeth Hospital was erected.

Chapter 6

Selly Oak Hospital

Organisation of the National Health Service
With the implementation the NHS Act of 1948, Selly Oak Hospital came under the supervision of the Birmingham Regional Hospital Board, one of fourteen boards set up in England and Wales. Each board had a duty 'generally to administer the hospital and specialist services in their area' which in the case of the Birmingham area was the counties of Herefordshire, Shropshire, Staffordshire, Warwickshire, and Worcestershire and the county boroughs within. This huge region was divided into twenty-six groups. Selly Oak Hospital was in Group 25 along with many other institutions: the Royal Orthopaedic, Canwell Hall Babies, Little Bromwich, Solihull, Catherine de Barnes, Lordswood Road Maternity, Sorrento Maternity, Midland Eastcote Grange, Moseley Hall for Children, Ronkswood and Swinfen Hall. The Administrative Office for Group 25 was, until 1974, at Oak Tree Lane, Selly Oak in the old casual wards, although by 1963 some administrative staff had moved to the newly built Arthur Thomson House on the Hagley Road in Edgbaston; the Birmingham Regional headquarters. Sir Albert Bradbeer, Lord Mayor of Birmingham 1947-1948, was vice-chairman of the Birmingham Regional Hospital Board until 1957. He was also chairman of the Selly Oak Hospital Management Board from 1948 until 1963. This influential gentleman also chaired a committee set up by the Central Health Services Council, the advisory body to the Ministry of Health. The report of this committee, which looked into hospital administration, was published in 1954 and became known as the 'The Bradbeer Report'. The report brought about a fundamental change in the running of hospitals with a management tripartite of a lay administrator, a senior doctor and the matron. A chief executive officer at group level, who it was specified would not be a doctor, submitted management decisions and had overall responsibility for implementing policies.

The National Health Service Reorganisation Act 1973

The NHS Reorganisation Act of 1973 along with the Local Government Act of 1972 was intended to bring about better co-ordination between health authorities and local authorities. The boundaries of area health authorities were matched to those of local authorities providing social services. The Birmingham Regional Hospital Board was replaced in 1974 by the West Midlands Regional Health Authority and the Birmingham Area Health Authority took over the administration of Selly Oak Hospital. Further changes occurred in 1982 when the whole Birmingham area was divided into five district health authorities, Central, East, North, West and South. The South Birmingham District Health Authority included Selly Oak and also Bartley Green, Billesly, Bournville, Brandwood, King's Norton, Longbridge, Moseley, Northfield and Weoley Castle. Behind this re-organisation was the notion that patients should come first and that local health services should serve their own communities and be managed by local people. Community Health Councils were established to give a voice for the people.

In 1989, the Regional Health Authority produced the 'Building a Healthy Birmingham' plan, which recommended re-location of the General Hospital and the Children's Hospital to the Queen Elizabeth site and the down grading of Selly Oak Hospital. This plan was abandoned at that time. However, in 1991 with the merger of the South and Central District Health Authorities some of the recommended changes did eventually happen. Reorganisation of the hospital services resulted in the closure of the Broad Street Orthopaedic Clinic in 1993 and of two major hospitals, the Accident Hospital in 1995 and the General Hospital in 1996. Both of these highly esteemed hospitals were in the Central District and had been at the centre of caring for those injured in the Birmingham bombings of 1974. The General Hospital was refurbished and became home to the Birmingham Children's Hospital which transferred there from Ladywood Middleway in 1995.

In 1997 the University Hospital Birmingham National Health Service Trust was formed and Selly Oak Hospital joined with the Queen Elizabeth Hospital. Foundation status was granted in 2006 and the hospitals jointly became known as the University Hospitals Birmingham NHS Foundation Trust. The introduction of foundation trusts was part of a government programme to create a 'patient-led NHS', the idea being that rather than central government making decisions about local health care the responsibility was devolved down to a local level, where the interests and needs of local people could be identified. With more local involvement there was no longer a need for Community Health Councils, which were abolished in 2003.

Selly Oak Hospital under the NHS

In 1948 with the introduction of the NHS, Mr. R.P.S. Kelman remained as medical superintendent of the Selly Oak Hospital; he was also a member of the Hospital Management Board. Honorary consultant physicians and surgeons were appointed to full or part time salaried posts and were permitted to retain the right to treat their private patients for fees.

Miss Brown, matron from 1953 until 1962, had the task of bringing together the two separate institutions of Selly Oak East (the hospital) and Selly Oak West (the former workhouse).

There was concern that there would not be sufficient nurses to provide care for the extra patients who were now eligible for free medical treatment. Most hospitals already had nurse training schools as it was in their own interest to train probationer nurses who were the major work force. One source of recruits was Ireland from where there had been a steady influx of girls since the 1930s. The main reason for this was that in Ireland they had to pay for their training whilst in England they paid no fees and received a small salary as well as their uniform, board and lodging. Selly Oak Hospital had a large contingent of Irish student nurses many of whom remained at the hospital once their training was complete, eventually becoming senior members of the nursing staff.

Over the years new departments were opened as the hospital service expanded and developed. The first of these was the Veitch Physiotherapy and Dental Department, named after Mr. T.N. Veitch, Vice-Chairman of Group 25. It was opened in 1951 and was situated close to F and E Blocks in the old laundry which had been disused since 1936. Miss Bridget Dixon, the superintendent physiotherapist, planned the conversion of the old buildings. Sixteen full time chartered physiotherapists were employed to treat out-patients and in-patients and to supervise the training of students from the Queen Elizabeth and the Royal Orthopaedic Hospitals.

The department was well equipped with provision for general physiotherapy, sunlight and radiant heat, short-wave diathermy, medico-electric treatment, wax treatment, remedial exercises and hydrotherapy. The same building also housed new dental facilities with two dental surgeries and a recovery room. There was a separate entrance and waiting hall, which it is recorded, had an aquarium 'to amuse children'.

The first hospital chapel was in a wooden hut situated between J and K Blocks and in 1954 a new chapel was dedicated. It was constructed in what had been an open corridor on the first floor of the main block. Services were held there regularly and it was also a quiet place for the use of staff and patients. The Friends of the Hospital provided funds to buy an altar rail and a baptismal bowl.

During the 1960s as the country began to experience more prosperity, finance for the health service became less of an issue and many hospitals were able to expand their services. Selly Oak Hospital was no exception and new operating theatres were opened in 1962.

Temporary theatres were constructed on Ward C1 whilst improvements to the existing theatres took place. They were remodelled and brought up to date with improved heating and ventilation systems and post-operative recovery rooms.

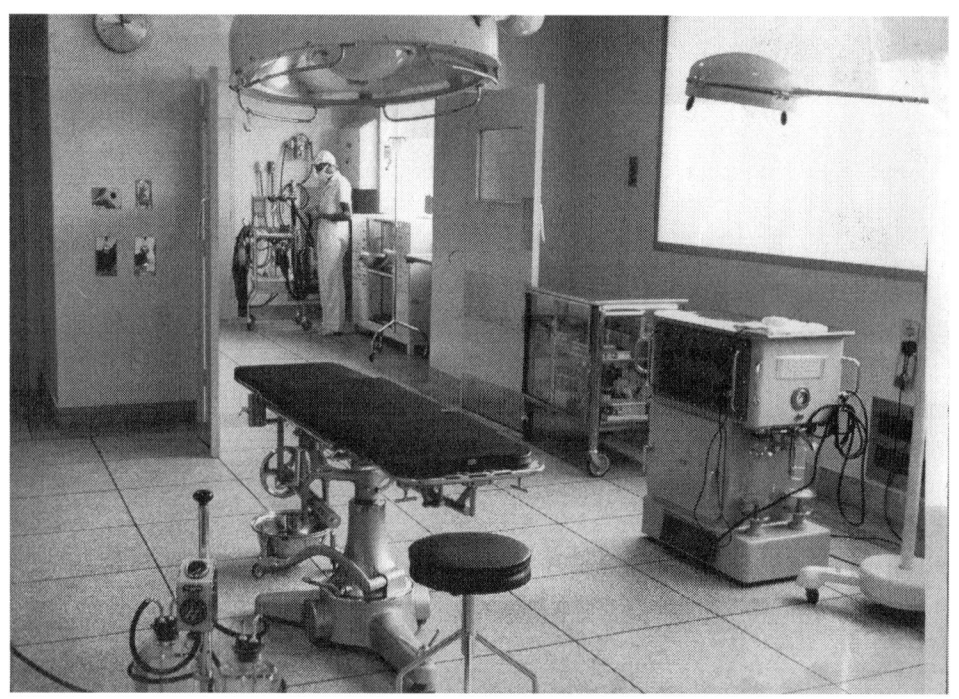

The New Operating Theatres 1962. (Photograph courtesy Medical Illustration – University Hospitals Birmingham NHS Foundation Trust)

The new twin theatres were entered through an air lock. Each theatre had its own anaesthetic room and scrub up facilities. Post-operative recovery cubicles, sterilising and wash up rooms were shared. The theatres were fitted with double windows, which had electrically operated blinds between the sheets of glass. There was an X-ray room, and illuminated screens to view X-ray plates were built into the theatre walls. A system of emergency lighting automatically came on should an electricity failure occur. There were improved autoclaving facilities and a specially designed preparation room with large store cupboards and benches for packing the drums for autoclaving. On the roof of the block, an air treatment plant supplied filtered, heated and humidified air to the theatres below. A record written by Sister McLaughlin, theatre sister at the time, declared the theatres a 'great success'.

A year later in 1963, the new out-patient department was opened. It was built on the site of Selly Oak Cottages, on the corner of Oak Tree Lane and Raddlebarn Road. During the 1930s and 40s, these cottages were home to the staff drivers, whose job it was to chauffeur senior medical staff.

The Out-Patient Department 1963. Walking Patients' Entrance Oak Tree Lane. (Picture taken from the Official Program for the Opening of the New Out-Patient Department. Birmingham Regional Hospital Board 1963)

The new facility was badly needed as the demand for out-patient services had doubled since 1949, when total attendances were 50,079, including 12,810 new patients. By 1962 there were 100,076 attendances of which 18,946 were new patients.

In the courtyard at the front of the building, facing onto Oak Tree Lane, a bronze sculpture was erected, representing 'Compassion'. Commissioned by the Foyle Trust, at the instigation of Sir Albert Bradbeer, it was the work of Mr. Uli Nimptsch. Outside the rear entrance, which was also the ambulance pick up point, was a building for ambulance staff. This building was later enlarged to house clerical staff and large quantities of patients' medical notes and X-rays.

The Ministry of Health issued a White Paper in 1962 that asked hospital management committees in England and Wales to develop their services by modifying current proposals and bringing forward new ones, which reflected the needs of their areas and the changing methods of medical care. Over the next three decades several proposals were put forward for the redevelopment of Selly Oak Hospital, none of which came to full fruition.

The Out-Patient Department 1963. Ambulance Approach from Raddlebarn Road. (Picture taken from the Official Program for the Opening of the New Out-Patient Department. Birmingham Regional Hospital Board 1963)

One such in 1966 was the development of a district general hospital at Rubery on the site of the mental hospital, and the redevelopment of Selly Oak Hospital as a centre for trauma and orthopaedics along with the Royal Orthopaedic Hospital. This proposal was rejected, however surviving details of the plan give an idea of the hospital at that time. Major concerns were the increasing number of patients, overcrowding, lack of beds, worries about the early discharge of patients and the morale of medical and nursing staff. The total number of beds was 856 with 325 for geriatrics, 499 for acute cases and 32 for obstetrics. Specialities included E.N.T (ear, nose and throat), paediatrics and special care babies, ophthalmology, obstetrics and gynaecology. The designation of the wards in the former workhouse and the infirmary is shown in **Table 9** and demonstrates some of the difficulties of adapting the old buildings.

In the proposal it was noted that the new out-patient department, which was opened only three years earlier, lacked flexibility for clinic use and that the X-ray and pathology facilities took up a lot of space. The plan states a need for new X-ray and accident departments, an occupational therapy department, a new pharmacy, an enlarged dining room and kitchen, a new linen store and more residential accommodation for the medical and nursing staff. It was suggested that Blocks M, F, L, the fracture clinic and the accident department should be demolished and furthermore that Blocks K, J and E along with the antenatal and dental clinics, physiotherapy and pathology departments should all be upgraded.

A car park was also planned to accommodate eight hundred cars. Within the proposal was a plan for a new sixty bed maternity unit.

This proposal was never fully implemented. Over the following years some recommendations were undertaken whilst others were implemented elsewhere, as in the instance of the maternity services, with a new block being erected next to the Queen Elizabeth Hospital. In 1969, the antenatal and obstetric services were transferred there from Selly Oak Hospital.

Table 9

**Birmingham Hospital Board –
Outline of Function
Selly Oak Redevelopment** (25/7/1966)

Ward Block	Number of beds	Allocation of beds	Floors	Remark
Old Infirmary Blocks				
A	98	Medical Wards, Children's surgical, Pharmacy	3 floors with lift	Needs upgrading
B	123 (incl Bridge Ward)	Surgical	2 floors with lift	Needs upgrading
C	123	Opthalmic Wards E.N.T. and Trauma Surgical and Medical 1 R/D Room	2 floors with lift	C1, C3 recently upgraded C2, C4 being upgraded
D	103 and 6 SCB Cots	Obstetric SCB Gynaecological Surgical	3 floors with lift	Needs upgrading
Old Workhouse Blocks				
M	132	Chronic Sick	3 floors with lift	A very narrow building which could not be upgraded to give reasonable accommodation
L	26	Children	2 floors no lift	Inadequate for ward accommodation
F	25	Children	2 floors no lift	Inadequate for ward accommodation
K	163	Surgical 23 Chronic Sick 140	2 floors with lift	In poor condition but could be successfully upgraded
J	68	Chronic Sick	2 floors with lift	Has been upgraded
E	72	Acute Medicine	2 floors with lift	Has been upgraded

Throughout the 1970s, the population of Selly Oak increased and there was concern about the lack of hospital beds to serve a population variously estimated between 320,000 and 450,000. To rectify this situation it was decided to build a new surgical block on the site of the tennis courts at the north-eastern side of the hospital. A turf cutting ceremony in May 1975 performed by Mr Bob Sage, consultant surgeon, marked the start of a £3 million building project by Taylor Woodrow Construction. It was completed in November 1976 when Dr. Raymond Blatchford, consultant physician, poured the last of the concrete at the topping out ceremony. This new four-storey building was connected to the main hospital by a long corridor. The opening of S Block, as it was known, added 232 beds to the 602 already on the site. At the same time four additional theatres were built which brought the total number of theatres to nine: eight for list cases and one for emergencies.

S Block. (Richard Daniels 2004)

When S Block was built a hospital sterile supply unit (HSSU) was set up on the ground floor and opened in 1978. The surgical supplies store had been housed, since the late 1960s, in West Lodge, once the workhouse gateway. Miss Joan Teasedale, who was theatre superintendent for many years, took over the management of the unit, and remembered that she *'was able to inaugurate a tray service for theatre. The instrument trays came out of theatre, my girls sorted them out and they went back to theatre through an airlock. We did the medical stores as well. It made sense. We knew the hospital. If someone made a mess, say a medical ward ordered three boxes of surgical gloves, you knew that wasn't right'*. Eventually in the 1990s, surgical and medical stores were ordered and delivered from a central depot at King's Norton.

K Block was refurbished in 1975 and the ground floor was turned into two new departments for the physiotherapy and occupational therapy services. The dining hall at the back of K Block was turned into a gymnasium and there was far more space than in the old physiotherapy block which had previously housed the hospital laundry. Both departments were well equipped and did much to speed the rehabilitation of in-patients besides treating many out-patients.

From the late 1960s there was a trend for different hospitals to focus on certain specialist services rather than provide an overall service. At Selly Oak Hospital, as well a providing the normal surgical and medical services, some specialist centres and units were set up which were directly linked to the medical school at Birmingham University. In 1969 the hospitals at Selly Oak, Dudley Road and East Birmingham were approached by the medical school and asked to provide facilities for teaching undergraduate medical students. It was apparent that with the rising numbers of medical students the facilities for clinical teaching were inadequate within the United Birmingham Hospital Group. Eventually all three hospitals were recognised and designated as University Teaching Hospitals. At Selly Oak Hospital facilities for undergraduate and post-graduate medical students were developed that eventually included a medical library and post-graduate lecture theatre, where regular meetings and lectures were held for medical students, hospital doctors, general practitioners and other health professionals such as nurses, physiotherapists, pharmacists and dieticians.

The Coronary Care Unit was opened in 1968. This new specialist unit had six beds for the advanced care of patients with myocardial infarction, and was under the supervision of Dr. R.E. Nagle. A medical registrar was awarded a Sheldon Fellowship to undertake research into the treatment of heart disease and at the end of the first year more than 400 patients had been treated. The unit was well equipped with all the latest monitoring devices and was eventually enlarged.

Birmingham University was granted a one hundred year lease on a piece of land close by K Block as the site for an academic centre. The Hayward Building was purpose built and opened in 1975 for the department of gerontology. It was here that Professor Bernard Isaacs of Birmingham University, who was given the first Charles Hayward chair of geriatric medicine, and his team undertook much of their research. They looked at the four 'I's' of old age, 'instability, immobility, intellectual impairment and incontinence' and one thousand 'elders' were enrolled in their studies. This resulted in the development of useful aids and implements designed to assist elderly and disabled people with daily living tasks.

In 1982 Professor Paul Bacon was appointed to the chair of rheumatology at the University of Birmingham. The rheumatology department was sited at the Medical School, the Queen Elizabeth Hospital and Selly Oak Hospital, and was for many years one of the foremost rheumatology centres in the country where revolutionary new therapies for the treatment of rheumatic diseases were researched. The Selly Oak Hospital management team encouraged the location of a second professorial department on the site, and in 1991 the whole of E Block was refurbished and became a dedicated clinical rheumatology unit. On the first floor were two wards each with twelve in-patient beds. The ground floor was used for out-patient and research clinics and also housed the hydrotherapy pool. This was a valuable facility provided by the Birmingham Arthritis Appeal Trust with money raised by the fund raising efforts of patients and staff. A multi-disciplinary team of doctors, nurses, physiotherapists, occupational therapists, dieticians, pharmacists and podiatrists worked together to treat patients with a variety of rheumatic conditions. The research they undertook resulted in the better understanding and treatment of these patients, in particular those with early onset rheumatoid arthritis.

In 1995 the Birmingham Accident Hospital, famous as a world leader in the field of burns and trauma, was closed. The specialist staff transferred to Selly Oak Hospital where a modern intensive care unit was developed in the old theatre complex on the ground floor between S Block and the main hospital building. A new accident and emergency department, with an adjacent helipad, was opened in 1995 in front of S Block. A team of trauma consultants treating seriously injured patients was led by Mr. Keith Porter, who was jointly appointed as a specialist at the Accident Hospital and Selly Oak Hospital in 1986. In 2005 he was appointed to the newly created chair of Clinical Traumatology at Birmingham University. The quality of the new trauma centre and the specialist medical and nursing staff, who were experts in trauma, burns, plastic surgery and intensive care, and also the close links to the University of Birmingham Medical School, were important in the decision by the Army to transfer the care of their civilian and armed forces personnel to Selly Oak Hospital. Professor Porter was knighted in the 2010 New Year's Honours List for services to the Armed Forces.

The Royal Centre for Defence Medicine (RCDM) was opened by the Princess Royal in 2001. Seven RCDM nurses had already joined the accident and emergency staff in 2000 and were soon followed by more nurses, doctors and therapists. Military staff who wore their own distinctive uniforms depending upon whether they served with the Army, Navy or Air Force, were fully integrated with the existing NHS staff to treat civilian and military patients. An adjacent helipad enabled the transfer of severely wounded personnel from Afghanistan and Iraq back to Selly Oak Hospital within twenty-four hours for specialist treatment.

In 1997 Selly Oak Hospital and the Queen Elizabeth Hospital merged to become the University Hospital Birmingham, which was then managed as an

The New Accident and Emergency Department. (Richard Daniels 2004)

County Air Ambulance at Selly Oak Hospital. (Richard Daniels 2004)

NHS Trust. From 2006 both hospitals were managed as an NHS Foundation Trust. The two hospitals provided services to more than half a million adults every year, employed nearly 7,000 staff and were home to regional centres for cancer, trauma, burns and plastic surgery, besides having the largest organ transplant programme in Europe.

Plans were made for the eventual closure of Selly Oak Hospital and the transfer of staff and services to the new Queen Elizabeth Hospital. In 2010 the transfer of the Accident and Emergency Service, including the RCDM was the first stage of this process. Other services followed with the eventual closure of all patient services at Selly Oak in 2012.

Chapter 7

Memories of Selly Oak Hospital

Selly Oak Hospital has marked important milestones, happy and sad, in many people's lives. The solid, red brick buildings were an essential part of the local landscape. They evoked nostalgic memories and also provided a sense of permanence and history. For members of staff it became another 'home' where they trained and worked, and built life long friendships. Those who were asked about their memories of the hospital remembered it as a friendly place, *'just like a village, where everyone knew everyone else'*. Despite the hard work and discipline, most enjoyed working there and fondly recalled the camaraderie that existed between all members of staff.

Twenty-four people, former nurses, clerical staff, physiotherapists, a retired porter, patients, and local residents shared their memories, good and bad, of the hospital. The taped interviews were studied and themes were drawn from them and were amalgamated to make cohesive stories. The memories cover the period from the 1920s until the end of the last century. The intention is to help readers conjure up a picture of the hospital before changes in patient care brought about by advances in pharmacology, medicine and surgery inevitably altered the way in which hospital services were organised.

Memories of Selly Oak Hospital

East and West Side	87
Being an In-Patient	90
Children in Hospital	93
Patient Care	95
Patients' Medical Records	97
Visiting	99
Being a Nurse	101
The New Out-Patient Department	115
M and K Blocks	116
Keeping the Hospital Clean	119
The Maids	121
The Porters	122
The Social Club and Sports Field	124
Smokey Joe's	125
The Harry Payne Pavilion	126
Green Spaces and Car Parks	127
The Laundry	128
Christmas	129
The Visit of Princess Elizabeth and the Duke of Edinburgh	131
The Friends of Selly Oak Hospital	133

East Side and West Side

A former nurse, who was ninety-nine year's old when interviewed, described the difference between the workhouse and infirmary, during the 1930s *'we didn't mix with the nurses from the west side at all. They wore a different uniform. Sometimes a patient was transferred from them to the hospital, if they needed surgery or any real medical care'.*

Furthermore *'that side'* was *'for old people'* and *'was just medical wards for the chronic sick. Chronic cases were sent over to the west. They couldn't be sent home. They had nowhere to go and no one in the family to look after them. They were looked after very well. The old men used to get up and dressed and you'd see them in the grounds'.*

The division and differences between the two establishments, the workhouse (sometimes confusingly called the infirmary) and the hospital, still existed with the introduction of the National Health Service, as two former nurses explained. *'The other side was called the west side, the infirmary. There was a separate matron on the other side. They were separate to us altogether. We didn't know the other side.'* A big difference was that *'the infirmary nurses were not nurses as we knew them, they were assistant nurses. Remember that you are talking about not specifically medical or surgical patients but going on from the old workhouse. There were nurses on the wards who had never passed exams'.* The only contact was *'we could walk across. Because we used to send patients from A and E, and in those days we didn't have an ambulance, and we used to put a mackintosh over the trolley when patients were transferred over to the chronic side'.* Besides which, *'the conditions weren't good, you're talking about Victorian buildings. They'd stood the test of time but they didn't have modern facilities'.* Moreover *'the west side nurses lived in a nurses' home, not the Woodlands, their matron lived over the arch as you are coming down Raddlebarn Road. When the NHS started in 1948 we were still separate then'.*

The eventual amalgamation of the workhouse and the infirmary took place in the early 1950s. *'The master and matron retired and that side all came under the hospital administration. The west side blocks joined the hospital later on, they belonged to the other side which was a separate hospital called the infirmary. Our side, the east side, was called Selly Oak Hospital.'*

Despite this joining together, there remained a division between the two sides, which was well remembered. The difference between the nurses on the west side and those on the east side still persisted and was keenly expressed. *'We never had any truck with the nurses from the west side. We were a stuck up lot.'* And although *'the trained staff wore the same uniform as us, they did not have probationers, but they did have assistant nurses'*. It appears that there was a definite 'them and us' situation. *'The two lots of staff didn't mix between the two. We didn't know them because we had separate living quarters. We did not have anything to do with that side not even when they became joined with the hospital.'*

It appears that the stigma attached to the workhouse extended to anyone, even children, who was associated with it. A local resident remembered in the 1940s *'going back to the workhouse, when you got to the main gate there was matron's house, if you walked round Raddlebarn Lane, we called it Workhouse Lane, you would often see the cots with children. As children, we were told that those were the naughty girls' babies'*. In other words these were illegitimate babies, which in those days carried a social stigma further reinforced by being in the workhouse.

The workhouse association was epitomised by the railings, which *'were about six foot high with spikes on'*. One local resident, who was born in 1928, remembered *'the railings. I used to think it was like a blooming prison'*. During the 1950s even though *'the railings between the infirmary and the hospital had gone by then'* some did remain around the original workhouse site. *'The railings came all the way down*

*The Porters' Lodge and Main Hospital Entrance Circa 1930s.
(Postcard courtesy of Mary Harding)*

to the West Lodge which was for the people who worked on that side. Remember there were a lot of people who worked on that side.'

Although the 'them' and 'us' attitude eventually disappeared amongst the staff at the hospital, the stigma of its early workhouse origins persisted into the early part of the 21st century, especially in the minds of older people.

This description of the last inmate from the workhouse, during the late 1920s, shows that for at least one person, the workhouse, however bad, had been and was still his home.

'There was an old man who sat in the porters' lodge at the main gate. He was old but reasonably dressed and shaved and he sold bundles of sticks. He was from the old infirmary. He was the last patient they had. He had nowhere to go and they couldn't send him off. He'd got a bed somewhere, I don't know where it was, possibly in the infirmary side, he wouldn't be on his own, perhaps some porters lived there. He hadn't any money, of course. He must have had a pension. I don't know where he got the wood from, but he used to make up these bundles of sticks and he used to sell them to visitors, going into the hospital, for a few coppers (old pennies). That went on for a year or two.'

Being an In-Patient

During most of the 20th century a hospital stay was a major event in people's lives. Following surgery and childbirth patients were confined to their beds for at least a week and the treatment of many medical conditions often required even longer periods of bed rest. Generally the pace of life was slower and patients were not expected to get better immediately. As many would return to poor living conditions it was common practice for patients to be sent to convalescent homes to ensure complete recovery before finally being allowed to return home.

Wards ran like clockwork on a strict daily routine. For the patients this helped to break up the monotonous day but for the nurses it was a constant race against the clock. Matron ruled the hospital and did her ward inspections at least once a day. A former patient who *'was in there during the war, when I was nineteen, to have my tonsils out'* described how *'when matron came round, my goodness me, the beds had to be just so and you couldn't move. You weren't allowed to put anything on the lockers'*. Another woman remembered that *'nothing at all was allowed on the bed – everything had to be put away in the lockers. When the doctors came round everything had to be extra tidy'*.

As one lady recalled from her mother's description of being in Selly Oak Hospital in 1923, food was an issue. *'My mum was in the end, the open air – the veranda. The only thing she didn't like was the food. She said it was horrible and there was a gypsy woman in the next bed who ate all mum's food. We lived in Heeley Road and my grandma used to bring my mum food. She couldn't eat the hospital food. She was happy enough in there but she just didn't like the food.'*

Nineteen years later this lady was herself admitted to Selly Oak and despite her mother's experience she found the food acceptable, which was surprising considering that it was wartime and food was strictly rationed. *'You took your ration book. If any visitors brought you in an egg, they (the nurses) would put your name on it and you would get it for breakfast one morning. There was always plenty of porridge, toast, butter and marmalade. The toast was already buttered but it was scantily spread. Occasionally you would get bacon. You had a drink in the morning, then there was soup and a cooked meal at lunch, soup and a cooked meal in the evening, and a sweet as well. You got a big dish of pudding, not like today – a little pastry. The best was* rhubarb crumble but mainly it was rice pudding or some sort of milk pudding. We always had a drink at night. Some patients did the drinks' trolley if they were well enough.' Recovering patients were encouraged to go round with the evening drinks, usually something milky such as Ovaltine or Horlicks. This helped them to get up and about and also assisted the hard-pressed nurses at a very busy time when patients were being settled for the night.

Ward sisters were generally regarded as being matter of fact, somewhat unsympathetic and stern disciplinarians. Sister's word was law and woe-betide any one who displeased her, be they nurse, junior doctor, patient or ward cleaner. One patient, who had gone into hospital in 1957 to have her baby certainly experienced the ward sister's displeasure. '*I was feeling rough and having pains and I said that I didn't want any lunch and the sister said, she was a bit of a hard woman, "You come and eat your lunch at the table". She was shouting down the ward at me and I wasn't feeling very well. I got to the table and it was lamb stew, now I love lamb stew, but unfortunately I was sick all over the table. You ought to have seen her face, she was really disgusted. I couldn't help it. I said I didn't feel well.*'

But it seems that not only could ward sisters be harsh, as the same lady found out. '*There was a lovely lady doctor, but the man (doctor) was horrible. He used to shout at everybody. He shouted at me the night Paul was born something terrible. I was seventy-two hours in labour. There were two beds in this little room and from the other bed, all I could hear was them smacking a baby and then it crying its eyes out and they would say to me "Here's another one. When are you going to do it?" I was glad that I had to have forceps in the end. I wasn't allowed on my feet for a week afterwards. Sister said when I was coming out, "You'll be back," and I said,"I won't." I never had any more. I'd waited five years.*'

However, this woman's later experiences in Selly Oak Hospital in the 1990s were more enjoyable. '*We used to go in the day room and play cards until late at night and then they used to put us to bed. The doctors used to come in late to put this tube thing in. They were lovely. I had a lovely time in there for my operations. My friend Jane and I did just as we liked.*' This was quite a change from 1975 when she had her baby and '*the lights went out early and you'd hear people either snoring or moaning*'.

It took several decades for the new NHS hospitals to shake off the old workhouse ways. Even in the late 1950s patients felt that they had lost their identity and their freedom. '*They take all your clothes away and you couldn't get out because the lodge was there, and the lodge man, and there were railings.*' As a further reminder of the workhouse days '*night-gowns, dressing gowns and slippers were provided, some of which were very shabby*'. One ward sister shouted down the ward "what's that woman doing in her own dressing gown. Get something else on her".

There was a further loss of dignity as described by one patient who was admitted during the war. *'It was horrible – we used to sit on bedpans in the open ward. They didn't have curtains but they used to put screens across the ward doors.'* Patients were still going through this mortifying and embarrassing experience in the late 1960s. A clinical nurse tutor recalled that *'there were not enough screens to go round, so one screen was put across the ward door. Sister often had to prevent doctors and consultants entering the ward during toilet rounds'*. Eventually all wards did have curtains around individual beds, which afforded patients some degree of privacy. Another patient also remembered bedpan rounds, *'the nurses used to don green gowns, warm the bedpans and holding five in each hand, dump one on each bed, and then go back to help those unable to get on or off by themselves'*. And a former nurse recalled that in the 1950s *'we used to thread toilet rolls in the tapes at the back of the gowns, so that when patients wanted any, they just pulled it off the back'*.

One person was in Selly Oak Hospital, at the age of sixteen from 1954 until 1959, with a bone infection. She was apprehensive about going into hospital as *'it was only for the old and they didn't come out'*. She was nursed on ward D1 and spent long periods of time, one of which lasted for two years, resting in bed and was not even allowed to get out for the toilet. She coped well with being stuck in bed and having only older women and busy nurses for company and in fact later became a nurse herself. She recalled that it was very busy and *'frequently beds were put up in the middle of the ward to cope with emergency cases'*.

Daily life must have seemed monotonous for the patients although matron's, sister's and doctors' rounds, bed making, bedpans, blanket baths, back care, wound dressings and meal times meant that there was always plenty of activity on the wards. Smoking was permitted at certain times of the day. However, as one nurse described it *'the men used to smoke in bed. They used to put the sheet right up over their heads and light up under the covers. They thought the smell was under the sheets but it wasn't'*. Smoking was allowed in the wards up until the 1990s, when the issue of smoking became controversial and it was banned throughout the hospital, except in smoking shelters erected in the hospital grounds.

In 1962 a leaflet for the 'Guidance of In-Patients' gave the information that the library trolley, organised by the Red Cross, visited the wards weekly, newspapers could be bought on the ward twice daily, the Women's Voluntary Service operated a trolley service to each ward on a weekly basis from which toiletries could be purchased, and a free barber service was available on the male wards. The same leaflet ends by explaining, somewhat bossily, that *'By accepting and observing the arrangements in the ward you will not only be easing the work of the medical and nursing staff but you will be helping them to restore both yourself and your fellow patients to good health in the shortest possible time'*.

Children in Hospital

Childhood hospital experiences were very clearly described. In the 1950s, one former patient had mastoiditis which at that time was a common and very painful condition caused by ear infections. Removal of the diseased parts of the mastoid bone was a regular, surgical operation. Today, this operation, like tonsillectomy, is rarely performed. After several episodes of mastoiditis a former patient, who was seven years old at that time, was eventually admitted. *'This was an emergency operation in the middle of the night when my mastoid erupted and pus was everywhere. I was rushed to hospital by ambulance.'* She was in *'for months'*, firstly on one of the A Wards and then in K Block, where she was the only child. When her wound was dressed *'it was very painful as the nurses pushed the bandage packing in, covered with that yellow stuff* (Acriflavine). *They then had to pull it out. The wound had to heal from below and not across'*. In 1952, when she was about seven or eight years old and still in hospital, the death of King George VI occurred. *'They put me in my navy blue coat, which I had worn for my father's funeral, and put a black band on the arm for mourning for the King and we all stood outside K Block to observe a minute's silence. Whether the nurses felt sorry for me, I don't know, but they allowed the gardeners to take me over to the greenhouses. I felt very happy and it took my mind off things.'*

At about the same time a boy of ten years old was *'taken ill with appendicitis, which got to be peritonitis. He was very, very ill. He was in a ward where they were all old gents. It was a shame and the first time we saw him, he was sat bolt upright and he had blond curls, loads of them, and his little face was so white. His stomach was padded and it was one mass of scars. It broke your heart to see him. He was in for about three months'*. A few years later, a girl of eleven was also admitted for acute peritonitis. *'I had the operation and had to stay in bed for ten days. We had to have all our meals in bed.'* One of her abiding memories was of penicillin injections. *'I didn't like them. Since I was at the top of the ward I could see the nurses coming with the trolley, so I used to hide. The lady in the bed next to me was in hospital because she had had her lip bitten off by her dog. She looked after me and taught me how to draw.'*

F Block stood to the north east of E Block and *'was a medical ward for children in the 1950s'*. It was away from the hustle and bustle of the main hospital in the comparative quiet of the old workhouse area and was latterly used by the works department. Many of the chronically sick children on that ward *'were very ill and a lot of them died'*. L Block, which was demolished, in the late 1980s, was for babies and young children. A former nurse recalled in the late 1940s *'a medical children's ward was over there on L Block. I was taken over by a physician to see the children. I can see this child now, who had only been fed on National Dried Milk and never had any orange juice or anything and remember, those things were available then, and it was just a "flop", which was what we called those poor floppy babies'*. Free orange juice and cod liver oil were available for young children during and after the Second World War.

By the 1980s children were no longer admitted to Selly Oak Hospital but to the Birmingham Children's Hospital on Ladywood Road, close to Five Ways in Edgbaston.

Patient Care

Probationers, nurses undergoing training, looked after the patients supervised by trained nurses. The ward sister had overall responsibility for ensuring that patients were properly cared for. Patient care was task-orientated and concentrated on cleanliness, comfort, rest and wholesome food.

Patients normally had a bath on admission and prior to surgery. Thereafter, junior nurses gave them a daily blanket bath in their beds until they were considered well enough to get up and bathe themselves. Blanket baths, or bed baths as they were also known, entailed the patient being wrapped in a warm flannelette sheet (blanket) and being washed from top to bottom. This involved the use of two flannels, one for the top half of the body and one for the lower, two towels, one for drying and one to preserve the patient's modesty. Nurses took great pride in having their patients looking clean and tidy, with their hair brushed and teeth cleaned, sitting or lying comfortably in a freshly made bed with clean linen.

One clinical tutor remembered, that whilst teaching on the ward in the 1970s, *'doing the perfect bed bath on a real patient, in the bed with a student, as taught in the school of nursing on a dummy. When the student had gone away, the patient said "could I just have a little word? That's the longest bed bath I've ever had and I didn't really like it".'* She had got very cold because the 'perfect' bath took so long. As often happened, what was taught was not always the most practical way to go about tasks.

Long periods of time spent in bed led to all sort of discomforts and one former patient who was in hospital during the war remembered *'it was October, an Indian summer and it was boiling hot at night and being on those rubber sheets, it was dreadful'*. Thick red rubber sheets protected the mattresses and it was one of the nurses' tasks to wash, disinfect and dust them with talcum powder to prevent them perishing. They were then hung in the sluice room until needed. Rubber sheets were replaced, during the 1960s with thin polythene mattress protectors and polythene draw sheets; narrow sheets tucked across the middle of the bed, underneath the patient's bottom, with a linen sheet on top. Making and tidying beds, straightening sheets and draw sheets and rearranging pillows were ongoing activities to ensure patients were comfortable and that they did not develop bed sores, which were seen as an indication of poor nursing care. To prevent bed sores 'back rounds' happened every three hours, when the nurses turned patients in their beds, and rubbed their pressure points; back, bottom, heels and elbows, with surgical spirit. As one former nurse put it *'If we had any old chronics, we used to be careful they didn't get bed sores'*.

It is hardly surprising that many patients suffered with constipation, especially when, before there were curtains around individual beds, patients sat on bedpans in full view of their fellows. Patients were asked every morning and evening whether they had had their bowels open. The replies, sometimes in great detail and not very edifying, were recorded with other observations, in the TPR (temperature, pulse and respiration) book. Aperients were given regularly to help patients 'to go', often with a daily dose of vitamins and supplements, such as iron tablets and malt extract. If matters became really difficult an enema would be administered, a procedure that involved a great deal of red rubber tubing connected to a funnel and quantities of green, liquid soap in warm water. This was routine before surgical operations and childbirth. By the 1980s enemas came in small polythene bags with nozzles, which were much easier to administer although a still somewhat embarrassing experience for the patient.

Care was taken to ensure that patients received the correct diet for their condition and that they drank plenty of fluids. During their training nurses were taught that food was essential to recovery and had to pass an invalid cookery exam. Those patients who were unable to eat, for instance stroke patients, were spoon-fed at meal times by a junior nurse. Before meal-times the probationer nurses were responsible for giving each patient a clean tray with cutlery and salt and pepper. At lunchtime, the ward sister stood at a heated food trolley and dished out food for individual patients who would be given either a normal or light diet. The latter was usually white fish or sweetbreads (the pancreas and thymus glands of lamb, beef or pork and considered to be easily digestible), and milk puddings such as semolina, rice or tapioca for dessert. After this they were then allowed to embark upon a light and finally a normal diet. The serving of food was taken very seriously. One nurse remembered *'windows were kept closed to keep the dinners warm'*. One sister always insisted that *'there was a double saucepan of milk on the cooker and she would mash it into the potatoes'*. Before the days of refrigerators, when a 'waste not want not' attitude prevailed nurses had to be resourceful. *'On the wards we had churns of milk, which we kept cool in the pantries. If it went off, the nurses made cream cheese.'*

From the 1990s patients were given printed menus to choose their food for the following day, and ward orderlies served them their pre-plated meals.

Patients' Medical Records (Notes)

It is hard to imagine, in these days of computerised records, how much time and energy was spent in finding and keeping patients' medical records or 'notes' up to date. What a headache this was for beleaguered clerks and secretaries. Without the patient's notes, especially those with chronic conditions, it was difficult to plan future treatment.

In the early days of King's Norton Union Infirmary 'diet cards attached to the head of the bed' were the only records that were kept. As time went by medical staff kept more extensive records and these were usually kept at the foot of the patient's bed. Later notes were kept in a trolley that was wheeled out during the doctors' ward rounds. From the 1960s, nurses kept a record of the treatment and condition of individual patients in a Kardex system, which was updated every day and night.

Patients' notes were only written up by the medical staff and were confidential. They were kept in brown manilla files, which also contained referral letters from general practitioners and copy letters sent to them from consultants, blood tests and other biochemical and pathology results, as well as the results of X-ray examinations and many other investigative procedures such as E.C.Gs, endoscopies and MR scans. Eventually during the 1990s as multi-disciplinary care became more common, para-medical staff wrote in the notes. Some patients, with chronic conditions had as many as three sets of bulky notes.

There was no central storage for notes and many were kept in basements and some even in the disused water tower. Behind the scenes an army of clerks and consultants' secretaries was caught up in the task of 'chasing notes'. When notes could not be found the hunt was on and some of the strange places where they were discovered were *'behind heating pipes, in doctors' cars, in X-Ray envelopes, taken home by students doing projects, and in one surgeon's case thrown out of the windows'*. One set were *'burnt when the registrar's car caught fire on the motorway'*. The medical registrar in question also had badly burnt feet. He had been taking the notes home to catch up on his dictation from a busy out-patient clinic.

Ward clerks were responsible for tracing and keeping notes up to date. The first ward clerk at Selly Oak Hospital was appointed in 1970. She received a *'mixed reception'* and found that *'some sisters preferred to do their own clerical work'*. On one ward *'I was not allowed into the office and had a desk and chair under the stairs. I was told to keep out of the way and spent most of my time sitting in the grounds doing bits and pieces of clerical work that Sister did not want to do'*. Eventually, she was accepted and allowed into the office to do all of the clerical work.

Clerks in the out-patient department not only had the task of locating notes for consultants' clinics but they also booked appointments. Generally patients were *'quiet and non-violent'*. One clerk enjoyed *'the personal touch and commiserating with distressed relatives'*. But as the paperwork increased *'no-one had time to foster a caring attitude'*. This was a sad state of affairs, for most clerks valued their jobs and enjoyed the contact with patients, relatives and visitors.

Visiting

Visiting rules and regulations were strict and in the early 1950s they were set out on a card, which was given to relatives when a patient was admitted to hospital. Numbers were restricted *'it was two to a bed, three perhaps if one waited outside'* and *'visiting was only allowed twice weekly'* on Wednesdays and Sundays. At one time entry was by ticket only as described by a porter, *'when people came visiting, there was a hut next door to the lodge. They queued down the road and we inspected the tickets'*.

Queuing was well remembered by several people, *'you could never go through the lodge unless it was actually visiting time. There was a huge gate across. Before the war there were huge iron gates'*. Visitors were allowed to go to the wards after *'going through a dark green door in the wall and waiting in a room just beyond'*. One person recalled that during the war *'visitors queued in the road by the wall. There was a bit of a veranda thing to keep people dry, it was outside on the pavement. At 7 o'clock the man would come out and he would let you through. Everybody was through like mad because it was only an hour and of course the time was taken out of your hour's visiting'*.

By the late 1950s matters had improved slightly *'things had changed. It was more relaxed but it was a funny thing, there wasn't more visiting. My husband would come Wednesday and Sunday, twice a week still. My son was born early Saturday morning and it was Sunday before my husband was allowed to come in'*. Another woman described feeling as if she was incarcerated because *'they wouldn't let fathers into maternity, only twice or three times a week for half an hour. I could just see them (*her husband and son*) beyond the railings'*.

It may have been that visiting times were more restricted on the maternity wards for on another ward *'visiting times were 2.30 pm to 3.30 pm on Sundays and Wednesdays and 7 pm to 7.30 pm every other day'*. Strict visiting times also applied to the parents of sick children. In those days visiting hours were seen as disruptive to the ward routine and upsetting for the children. *'Mothers would stand outside the railings for a glimpse of their children on A1 and wave to them.'* For children and parents alike the separation must have been extremely hard to bear. *'My mom and dad used to arrive early to be at the front of the queue so that they could spend the full hour with me. Visitors were not allowed to sit on the bed.'* One woman, who was an in-patient when she was a child, recalled that visitors were very important to her.

'What I would have done without visitors, I don't know. My mother, because she was working, arranged for her friends to come on a Wednesday afternoon and she would come on alternate Sundays, as she had to visit my father, who had TB, in Malvern on the other Sunday.'

In 1935, as an eleven year old, one woman remembered standing outside the hospital when her brother was born and gazing through the railings. Occasionally she was lucky to catch sight of her mother who came to the window to wave. One person managed to get beyond the railings in order to see *'Mrs. Rose, a neighbour. I went to visit her and had to stand on my toes to look through the window and speak to her'*. During the war one woman visited her father, who had tuberculosis and was nursed on ward B3 for several months. *'Because he agreed to be in a side ward with a young man of twenty with cancer, whose leg had been amputated, he was permitted regular visits.'* However, because she was a child, she was only allowed to see him once. A little boy whose mother was unable to visit him, as *'she was in bed having a baby'*, had visits from his sister instead, who *'was only thirteen and you were supposed to be fourteen. I used to worry myself sick and used go and be very quick and quiet in case I got told off'*.

Receiving flowers was an important part of being in hospital especially for the women. *'Lots of neighbours sent me flowers that they had picked out of their gardens and wrapped in newspaper.'* The flowers were for everyone on the ward to enjoy and comment on. During the 1950s and 60s *'flowers weren't put on your locker they were put on the central table. They took them out at night and brought them back in the morning'*. One former nurse tells of a ward sister who was in charge of a men's ward, who picked flowers from the hospital garden *'otherwise there would have been no flowers'*. Some ward sisters arranged and cared for the flowers but, in later years, this task was undertaken by ward orderlies. *'Somebody always did the flowers every morning.'* However as one person remarked *'they don't take them out at all and sometimes the flowers are so dead and still in a vase. I think it looks scruffy'*. This no longer happens in hospitals where there generally appears to be a 'No Flowers' policy.

Before visitors were admitted to the ward everything had to be tidy, including the patients. The nurses went round and tidied the beds, made sure that the patients were comfortable and set chairs out by each bed. A hand bell was rung to mark the end of visiting time and quiet would return for a short time before the routine of pressure care and bedpan rounds was resumed.

The rules about visiting had become rather lax according to one lady whose husband was admitted to J Block in 1985. *'There was a gentleman in bed with a crowd around. You are only supposed to have two or three at the most.'* Today, whilst restrictions still apply to visitor numbers, on some wards set visiting hours are a thing of the past.

Being a Nurse

The following memories of nursing at Selly Oak Hospital cover the decades from 1920s until 1990s. Four of the eight nurses who were interviewed also trained there.

Nurses had been trained at Selly Oak since 1897, but it wasn't until 1922 that a sister tutor was appointed, followed several years later in 1938 by the appointment of a maternity sister tutor to train pupil midwives. In 1942, the Amy Bodley School of Nursing for the training of registered nurses was opened in the original workhouse entrance block. Miss Bodley, who was matron from 1913 until 1938, was a forceful member of the Poor Law Infirmary Matrons' Association and did much to promote the training of poor law nurses.

In 1947 male student nurses were accepted for training. Student midwives (Part One) and pupil assistant nurses (State Enrolled Nurses) were also recruited. Pupil assistant nurses were taught in School Number Two, the former sewing room next to the linen room. In both schools lectures were given by sister tutors, consultant physicians and surgeons and specialists from other disciplines such as radiography, biochemistry, pharmacy, physiotherapy and dietetics. Sisters and clinical tutors taught probationer and pupil nurses on the wards. Student nurses and midwives lived in the Woodlands Nurses' Home and pupil assistant nurses in the Springfield Nurses' Home, which was built in 1947 on Raddlebarn Road, opposite West Lodge.

In 1969 the first clinical teacher was appointed to work on the wards alongside nursing staff. Eventually there were three clinical teachers, whose job it was to bridge the gap between the ward and the school and help initiate good nursing practice across the hospital. The training of nurses continued at Selly Oak until the early 1990s when Project 2000 was set up by the UKCC, (the United Kingdom Central Council for Nursing, Midwifery and Health Visiting). Nurse education was then transferred to the Further Education College in Westbourne Road, Edgbaston where nursing and midwifery courses were taught to degree level. The nurses' training school closed and student nurses were rarely seen on the wards. Today nursing assistants are responsible for the basic care of patients, whilst registered nurses deal with the more specialised aspects of nursing care.

Prior to the 1990s, hospitals were reliant upon large numbers of student nurses to look after the patients' basic needs. One former nurse felt that *'there is not the hands on nursing care that there was. We were more caring. They haven't got the same contact which is sad'*. Another observed that nursing *'is not the same. We had more contact with patients. They were in for longer periods and you got to know them and they got to know you. Now the turnover is so much quicker and it's like a conveyor belt'*.

Nursing was for many decades a popular profession for young girls to enter. Apart from nursing, teaching or secretarial work, few job opportunities existed for educated girls. Parents were comfortable about their daughters leaving home as during their training students lived in the nurses' home, where the home sister enforced strict rules. After training, a qualified and registered nurse was able to work anywhere that she chose. Some registered nurses elected to continue training and qualified as midwives thus giving them further skills and opportunities. Up until the Second World War probationer nurses were not accepted without having had some previous experience and they were generally older. *'I started my training at Selly Oak Hospital in 1930 when I was twenty five. Previously I had worked for five years at the National Children's Home and Orphanage at Sutton Coldfield.'*

Prospective nurses were able to choose where they wanted to train. One described her experience in 1946. *'My local hospitals were Selly Oak and the Queen Elizabeth. I chose to train at Selly Oak as it was just around the corner and I could start sooner.'* This particular nurse could not wait to get started, *'Queen Elizabeth wouldn't take you before you were eighteen. At Selly Oak they were prepared to take you a bit sooner. I went along for an interview and Matron Poole said I wasn't big enough. I weighed only seven stone, and was small and thin. I was devastated. She said she would only consider me if I could get more robust'*. She was delighted when a few months later *'I started when I was eighteen'*.

Another nurse who trained during the 1940s, *'had no idea why I chose Selly Oak, because I originally wanted to be a doctor'*. But as *'there were only twenty places for women in the medical school out of one hundred and I couldn't guarantee getting a scholarship'* she chose nursing despite her mother saying *'it's hard work, you won't have any time, you won't have any money'*. Yet her family *'were proud that she had chosen to be a nurse'* and luckily *'my grandmother didn't mind because she didn't associate the hospital with the workhouse infirmary'*.

There was a strict nursing hierarchy with matron, who was usually supported by an assistant matron, being responsible for adequate numbers of trained and student nurses to run the hospital. Ward sisters organised the daily work on the wards. Senior and junior staff nurses looked after the patients and taught student nurses, who were known as third, second and first years. The status and seniority of the nurses was very important and shown by the *'different colours for different ranks, and starched aprons and caps'*. Nurses' caps came in all shapes and sizes, depending upon rank. They were made from stiffly starched, flat pieces of cotton, sometimes edged with lace for the senior nurses, which were made up into the required shape and held together with a safety pin. Sisters sometimes wore cotton strings under their caps tied underneath the chin. In the 1930s first year nurses wore *'a deep pink dress, with a very long gathered skirt which had three tucks for letting down'*. One nurse remembered that when she trained in the 1950s, *'the first three months were probation and we wore a pink uniform. After three months you went into a mauve uniform and each year you got a stripe, which was a white piece of tape, which was put on your right sleeve until you became a third year. The stripes on our sleeves denoted how long we had been in training'*. The senior nurses wore different uniforms, *'Matron wore navy with lots of buttons down the front. Assistant matrons wore aprons and bonnety sort of hats. Sisters who had been QAs (Queen Alexandra Nursing Corps) wore their army squares. Such a lot of them had been in the war'*. Another nurse remembered, *'staff nurses wore pale blue, sisters wore royal blue and assistant matrons and matron wore navy'*. Further distinctions for qualified staff were *'belts and buckles. You bought your own buckle when you were trained'*. Buckles were made of silver and attached to a wide piece of navy blue, stiff buckram. Furthermore *'all trained staff had starched cuffs, which you put on to go to the dining room, down the corridor or when Matron or consultants did ward rounds'*. The use of cuffs was discontinued in the 1960s. All nurses wore stiffly starched aprons, which they changed daily and always took off for meal times *'you changed when you went to lunch. We had straps at the back'*. Aprons were spotlessly clean and if they became soiled were changed immediately.

The uniform rules were strict during the 1940s, 50s and 60s. *'In those days, the nurses couldn't go out in the street in their uniforms.'* One nurse remembered that, *'we couldn't go out in uniform only along Raddlebarn Road. We only had cloaks not outdoor coats'*. Long, navy blue cloaks with red linings were provided for walking between the wards, the nurses' home and different departments and were essential, especially in the winter.

Nationally, during the 1980s, uniforms changed and became less formal. Nurses still wore dresses but with shorter skirts. The starched, white cotton aprons were replaced with disposable plastic ones, which were removed and put in the bin after the nurse had dealt with each patient. This was more hygienic and resulted in less work for the hospital laundry. Starched caps were replaced by white paper ones and eventually were no longer worn.

The Woodlands Nurses' Home was well remembered which was not surprising as it had been home for several years to all of the nurses who were interviewed.

As new probationers, they all had to report there on their first day. *'We all had to be there by a certain time. Home sister showed us to our rooms. There was a bundle of uniforms made up to our previously sent in measurements. We changed and then were taken down to the sitting room and were introduced to a nurse who showed us how to make up the cap.'* From the 1950s all student nurses started at the preliminary training school, which opened at West Bromwich Hospital where they resided for the first three months of their training before transferring to Selly Oak Hospital.

The Woodlands Nurses' Home. (Richard Daniels 2004)

Until the 1970s, *'all nursing staff lived in the Woodlands. Sisters occupied the top floor of one wing. All nurses had to report for their letters and sign in and out on their days off. There were separate dining rooms and sitting rooms for the nurses and sisters. Married nurses were not employed'*. Discipline was strict and home sister was always around. *'We had an electric kettle to make ourselves a drink and when we heard her coming we used to unplug it and put it in the cupboard – it's a wonder we didn't set fire to ourselves.'* Besides which *'it was cold in the Woodlands. There was central heating but no carpets. It was always cold'*. The nurses had to keep their bedrooms tidy, make their beds and change the linen. *'A clean sheet and a towel were put outside your room once a week by home sister. You put your dirty sheet and towel outside your room for the cleaners to bag up and send to the laundry.'*

The working day started early when *'one of the maids came in and went round with a bell along the corridors to wake the nurses up. Breakfast was at 7.00am. You went to breakfast in the main dining room and there was a roll-call'* held by *'an assistant matron, who sat at a table just inside the dining room door'*. Everyone *'stood behind their chairs until matron or night sister, had said grace; this was followed by a great noise as the wooden chairs were pulled out scraping the floor. Then they sat down at* tables, covered with white starched cloths, and were waited on by maids'. Breakfast was cooked 'it might be kippers or scrambled eggs, porridge and cereal'. Unfortunately 'if you weren't in and the doors were shut you'd had it, you didn't get your breakfast. You had to go straight onto the wards', but before that 'you had to excuse yourself to night sister', who 'would ring the nurses' home if you didn't turn up, if you were ill or slept in'.

One nurse remembered that during the 1920s 'every night we went into prayers at 9pm. I am not sure about Sundays. You would dodge it if you could, as a lot of them did. Home sister read a prayer. I agreed with it. As soon as she walked in you all had to stand and turn round and kneel with your arms on your chair seat with your hands together. Home sister wasn't always very punctual so we would all sit there. We used to chat. I once had thirteen boxes of chocolates in my wardrobe. Patients' visitors used to bring them in. If we all got together I would open one and we would eat our favourites and leave the rest for the cleaners'. It is no surprise that chocolate was so plentiful as Bournville model village, home to the Cadbury chocolate factory and its many employees, was only down the road.

One new student nurse described her first experience of food at the Woodlands in 1945. 'We went to supper and I nearly went home because it was steamed white fish followed by semolina.' Another nurse found that 'the food was alright really' even though it was immediately after the war when 'ration books were handed in'. Being under eighteen 'I was given bananas' a rare commodity in those days. During and for a while after the war 'you had a blue ration book. Every week you got your butter (2 ounces) in a jar and you had a jar for your sugar (8 ounces) and you carried these around with you' and then 'kept them in the ward pantry'. On Friday 'it was fish all day'. There were ways of filling up hungry, young women 'at the mid-morning break a big bowl of dripping and two loaves were set out with a big pot of tea in the hospital dining room'. If they were lucky 'sometimes we had cucumber or sandwich spread sandwiches'.

Those fortunate enough to have a day off could ask for 'breakfast in bed and a maid brought them a tray with cooked breakfast, toast and marmalade and a silver pot of tea with silver milk-jug and sugar bowl'. Also on a day off 'as a student you had to go to the hospital for lunch'. Evening meals varied, 'supper was at half past eight. It was a proper meal, something like pork pie and salad. It was the chef's favourite'. Sometimes 'we used to have tripe and onions and rabbit stew because it was after the war'. Seniority bought some benefits. 'When you were a sister you could talk to the chef and tell him what you liked.' What is more 'senior sisters had a dining room across the corridor from the main dining room'.

During the 1970s a home warden, who was not a nurse, was in charge of the Woodlands. As one former clinical tutor described it 'things got more liberal and *the school was no longer responsible for the young nurses'*. Gone were the days when home sister's eagle eye was everywhere and no longer were there strict rules within the nurses' home. *'Nurses were inviting their boyfriends to their rooms.'* This would have been unthinkable in previous years.

There were other changes for nurses during this decade. They received pay rises of, in some cases 30%, and no longer received free board and lodging. All nurses, whether they lived in the nurses' home or not, had to pay for their own food. From then onwards student nurses generally chose to live outside the hospital and eventually the Woodlands was no longer used as a nurses' home.

Nurses learnt much through their practical experience whilst working on the wards. As one nurse put it *'you went around the wards and you talked to patients and although you didn't realise it you were observing'*. The same nurse, as a very junior probationer, observing that a patient was very unwell, and as she *'didn't know what was wrong, walked smartly up the ward to sister, you could only run if it was haemorrhage, fire or sudden death'* and *'sister and staff nurse were in the ward before I had finished speaking. The patient was a diabetic and was going into a coma'*. That nurse *'had never forgotten that you only learn by going around and talking to people'*.

Whilst the practical aspects of nursing were taught on the wards by the senior nursing staff, and later in the 1960s and 1970s by clinical nurse teachers, the academic side was taught in the school of nursing by nurse tutors. During the 1930s, *'between the entrance to the workhouse and our entrance there was a building that was turned into lecture rooms during my training. The home sister was our sister tutor. You had to pass her window and it might be slightly open and the curtains drawn back. If she wanted to see a nurse then she would call her name out to be sure to catch her. After a teaching lecture, you had to write it out and hand your book into her every week and she used to mark it. She put the book on a little table outside her room and if your book wasn't there you had to knock at her door. She'd go right through the lecture with you and tell you off for not writing better and about your spelling'*.

Physicians and surgeons also gave lectures but one surgeon, in the late 1920s, imparted knowledge to a junior probationer more informally. *'Mr. Baird was a general surgeon, he was old but I liked him. When you were sitting by an empty trolley in the anaesthetic room and weren't busy making dressings, he would sit on a stool and tell you about operations. We learnt a lot. One day he said to me "I've got a book you would be interested in about surgery", so he bought me the book and said, "Now you read up all the operations you've seen and see how much you recognise". I took the book and read and read and learnt a lot.'*

During 1940s Miss Brown was the sister tutor. *'We were frightened of her, she was very strict but very good. We had lectures at 9 o'clock in the morning or a 5 o'clock lecture in the evening and, very often when we came off night duty, we had a 9 o'clock lecture in the morning.'* It was common practice for night nurses to attend lectures during the daytime when they would want to be sleeping and how they were expected to learn anything after a night working on the wards is unimaginable.

Student nurses spent three months on each ward, which meant that by the end of their training they would have worked in every speciality. New probationers were introduced immediately to the wards. *'You were told at breakfast about any changes and which ward you would be on. The list went up in the dining room. We went on at 7.30am and you had to clock in. Everybody clocked in, all the nurses, trained and probationers, in the lodge.'* This did not leave much time to have breakfast and report for duty on the ward.

It was hard work on the wards. *'You just did as you were told as a probationer; bedpans and all the dusting, back rounds three times a day.'* However, *'the cleaners knew everything about the wards and as a junior nurse they told you what to do and what not to do. Discipline on the wards was very strict. One instance was that, when the wards were cleaned, all the central wheels at the foot of the black iron beds had to be set at exactly the same angle. By the time sister came on the ward, it had been damp dusted and the patients were sitting upright looking immaculate, the corners done properly and the beds straight, the curtains drawn and pleated. Sister would run her fingers over the surfaces to see if they had been dusted'.* Dust was always a problem especially as many of the wards had *'coke fires'* even though the hospital was equipped with central heating with *'no pipes showing, they were under the floor'* other forms of heat were needed. *'There were two big stoves one nearer the door and the other at the end of the ward.'* On other wards things were different *'there were coal fires in the middle of the wards. They were nice when you were on night duty but you had to fetch the buckets of coal of course'.*

Giving medicines and injections were one of the main tasks of the senior nursing staff. Junior nurses *'had to go down, for the drug orders, to the dispensary. We had a wicker basket for routine lotions and medicines. There was also the Dangerous Drug Book'.* This was a record of the amounts and times that drugs, such as morphine, were administered and to whom. Three times a day a senior nurse did the drug round with a junior nurse to check the drugs and dosages against each patient's records. After the war, some new drugs were introduced with strict precautions. *'I remember when streptomycin came in and we had to put on gloves and gown and mask to give it.'* And *'penicillin wasn't given by mouth because it was thought that the gastric juices would destroy it. We gave 20,000 units three hourly by injection'.* One nurse described how *'the ward sister did a lot of things in those days. Before we went off in the evening, we would have given out a lot of things that sister had decided upon, such as analgesia, because she knew what the surgeon liked'.*

Senior nurses were also responsible for the daily dressing of wounds. Night nurses laid the procedure and dressing trolleys up ready for the day nurses who would only have to add instruments, which were boiled in sterilizers on the ward. Nurses also undertook laying out their dead patients, which could be upsetting especially as they often knew the dead person very well since they had probably cared for them for a number of weeks. Two nurses, a senior and a junior took on the task. The body was washed and dried carefully, hair was brushed and all orifices plugged with cotton wool. Then a shroud was put on and the whole body wrapped in a winding sheet and the patient's name pinned onto the front. As one nurse put it *'last offices – you always tried to make them look good'*. After all it was the last thing that could be done for the patient and it had to be done properly. The porters then took the body to the mortuary in a covered trolley. When children died it was devastating, *'we always tried to find a few flowers for a child'*. Nurses would put the flowers in the child's hands, which were crossed on the breast.

Matron commanded tremendous respect and to take her around the ward was a terrifying prospect for new probationer nurses. During the day *'if sister wasn't there, then you had to take matron round and tell her what was the matter with each patient'*. Nurses were expected to know the names and conditions of every patient on the ward. Often senior nurses could be unkind and even petty minded especially if they thought that a nurse was insubordinate. While *'looking after an elderly patient in a side ward'* one nurse was told by an assistant matron to *'report to matron at 9.30am'*. When she questioned this she was told, *'don't be insolent'*. The assistant matron then walked around the ward and finally put the lights off and gave the reason *'for leaving the lights on'*.

Generally student nurses accepted discipline without question even if it meant running errands during their meal breaks. *'If you broke a cup or there was a breakage on the ward, you had to put it on a little tray, enter it into a book and take it to the assistant matron's office where she signed and you had to take it down to the basement to get rid of it. That was in your lunch break. If there were any forms to go to the pathological department you had to take those and deliver them.'* Someone had to account for the expense of breakages *'one sister insisted on an inventory being taken every evening. The thermometers and spoons had to be counted'*.

Although eating on the ward was forbidden, most nurses could not resist the temptation of finishing uneaten food. One nurse, who had missed her dinner, spoke of an incident when she decided to go behind the kitchen door to eat some of *'the rice pudding, which was always delicious'*. Matron suddenly appeared on the ward so the bowl with the rice pudding was hidden in the roller towel behind the door. Later another nurse went to dry her hands and the pudding ended up on the kitchen floor. Of course it made a terrible mess but the *'worst thing ever was to be caught out'* which, luckily, she wasn't. However, one morning *'a dare devil Irish nurse'* was not so fortunate when she decided *'to cook poached egg on toast for all the nurses on duty, having first got one of the porters to go down to the main kitchens for some eggs. She wouldn't have dared if sister or staff nurse had been on duty. The nurses were going into the kitchen one at a time to have their eggs'* when Matron Amy Bodley, who *'would turn up at any time'* appeared. She made the nurse scrape *'all the eggs and toast, that were in the oven keeping warm into the pig buckets. The nurse was told off on the ward but had to go down to Matron's office for a further scolding'*.

Doctors' rounds were serious affairs. They were conducted slowly and quietly with the ward sister and at least one other nurse in attendance. A former nurse remembered *'one Irish ward sister who had been there for years'*, who was extremely strict especially during the consultant's round. It had to be very quiet as if *'God was walking around – absolute silence'*. The ward was closed *'doctors did a round and the ward doors were kept shut and there had to be complete quiet'*. Before the days of curtains around each bed, *'when the doctors went round there was always a nurse who moved the screens around from bed to bed'*. In those days *'there were no doctor's bleeps. Outside every ward there were three lights: red, green and yellow. When the doctors were doing their round and the ward doors were closed, there was silence. The most junior nurse would stand by the light above the phone. If the light flashed you rang the switchboard and asked if there was a message for one of the doctors'*.

Student nurses did three months day duty and then three months night duty throughout their training. *'On night duty it was three months on with two nights off in the week.'* As a former nurse remembered, *'you worked three weeks before you got two nights off. Generally it was every week but it wasn't regular, it depended'*. Another recalled, *'it could be difficult to get off night duty and some nurses did nearly six months at a stretch'* and that *'the night staff came on at 8 pm and finished at 8 am'*.

Being on night duty brought great responsibility for senior student nurses. *'When I was a third year I was in charge of the ward at night and I sometimes had a junior. You didn't always get a junior for just your ward. Sometimes she had to act as a runner between two wards. We had a third year in charge, not probationers, but no trained staff apart from the night sisters.'* It was reassuring that night sister would visit each ward during the night. *'Night sister did her rounds between 9 and 11 at night and then again between 2.30-3.00am and 6.30 in the morning.'* Another nurse remembered, *'night sister went round with the night nurses'* and yet another recalled *'in my day night sister went round and had a word with every new patient'*. During the 1930s *'we used the kitchen as our office at night. There was a white cloth put over the scrubbed table'*. Usually night nurses came onto a quiet ward with the patients ready to sleep. 'Miss Malcolm, the night superintendent, was very strict. She did not allow any lights on in the wards.'

On most wards, as well as patient care, there were chores for the staff throughout the night. *'When the night nurses came on duty, their first job was to drape the procedure trolleys with green towels and lay them up with the required equipment. Every night they packed sterilising drums with dressings. The iron clipboards for patients' notes were the right size for making dressings. Gauze was wrapped around them and then cut and packed into drums along with cotton wool balls. These were made by placing great wads of cotton wool on top of the hot sterilizing boilers to fluff up, layers of cotton wool were peeled off and made into balls. Porters collected the drums and wheeled them on a trolley to the autoclave near to K Block. The sterilised drums were delivered back the next morning.'*

One nurse in the 1930s managed to have some relaxation during the long night. *'My favourite time was when everything was quiet and they were all asleep. I used to go and sit in an armchair, a wooden one with cushions in, and do my knitting. We might have an hour. We kept quiet because you didn't want to disturb the men, if you did they would then start wanting bottles and then you would have to do a round. We would always get them what they asked for. I would always do my duties well.'* But one nurse, in the 1950s, was aware of the night superintendent, who *'would creep around spying on the nurses. She would feel the kettle to see if it had been boiled recently and if it was warm she would accuse them of drinking tea'*.

Another job for one night nurse, during the 1930s, was to cook a meal for the night sisters. *'Chicken and vegetables were left in baskets on the ward.'* Then in the early morning *'we buttered ready sliced bread and boiled the eggs for the patients' breakfast'* and on one ward the eggs were cooked *'in a linen bag and the middle ones were always runny'*. There was a lot to do *'before the day staff came on we had to do the waking up, bedpans, washes, and TPRs (temperature, pulse and respirations). The senior nurse would write the reports'*. Then *'Sister came on and did a round with the senior night nurse seeing every patient "Good morning, how are you today"'*.

The night nurses' world was turned upside down. *'On night duty you didn't get breakfast, you got your dinner – stew at 8 o'clock in the morning!'* Then of course it was a question of trying to get some sleep during the day. Often night nurses were given bedrooms on the top floor of the nurses' home where it was quieter.

All student nurses took a stint in the operating theatres. In the 1950s *'theatres were at the very end of the main corridor. That was the "holy of holies". There were two theatres: the big main one and a smaller one. At the end was a big shelf, we called "the altar", which had a curtain around and underneath were kept all the oxygen cylinders'*. The experience of working in theatre made a lasting impression on those who trained during the 1950s and 1960s. *'Everyone dreaded the call to main theatres* because we had a terror of a theatre sister.' Another former nurse described the theatre sister 'she was a very fierce, tall Irish lady who became very deaf' yet 'was the most inventive, wonderful person. She was very strict and she would tell you "not 99% a 100". We used to go up to the theatre from the ward with the patient and then stayed with them. You'd ask Basil or Smith, the two theatre porters, "What's she like today?" Basil would say, "she's in a foul mood this morning". You would go up there shaking.'

Nurses accompanied their patients to the operating theatre and often stayed throughout the operation. 'The ward nurses had to hold the retractor for the surgeon so they could take the tonsils out' and 'the surgeon would be saying "don't shake, don't shake". You never dared go out in the evening because you stank of ether.' A graphic description given by another nurse who 'was chiefly the third nurse, that is the one that is left holding the leg after it had been detached. I nearly had a fit – it was the weight of it. Things like that stand out although it's seventy years ago'.

One nurse, who became theatre superintendant, had many anecdotes of her time in theatres. 'The surgeons had to have the good gloves and the assistants and nurses had mended ones. I patched gloves until I could have dropped.' She also 'worked with one surgeon who had hands like spades yet he was such a delicate surgeon. I remember him saying, "Don't put all those, great, big horrible instruments out", and I would say, "You can't do a Caesar (Caesarean) with five inch dissecting forceps" but he did!' Her job was busy, 'in 1978 another four theatres were added, so we ended up with eight. You ended up like a policeman on the door to make sure that everyone got the right patient'. She 'didn't have the freedom that you had just as a theatre sister', but she 'tried to take a couple or three lists a week. I always took the new surgeons, because it was important to get to know them'. State Enrolled Nurses (SENs), as well as student nurses, also worked in theatres from about 1947. 'They were always there, we attracted a lot of ladies in their forties. They had brought up a family and didn't go into a panic when anything happened. One of the surgeons would say, "give me a green belt (SEN), she knows what I want".'

Another nurse remembered that 'in theatre you'd got great bales of gauze to make the swabs up into bundles of 12 tied up with tapes. Square abdominal mops had rings which had to be checked in case they were left inside'. These would be packed into 'the drums at night and then they were collected and taken up to the main theatre. The night nurse on theatres had to switch the autoclaves on in the morning at about six o'clock. The towels, gowns, everything was autoclaved'. But that wasn't the end of it, 'we cleaned theatres out, we washed the floor it was terrazzo tiling and there was a little red channel all round. We used to polish it with red cardinal polish'. Furthermore 'the sharp instruments were put into surgical spirit and the others were put into formaldehyde jars, with silver lids and we had to silver polish them. We had one big glass cupboard where the special instruments were kept for things like bone operations'.

Also *'we had sterilizers for big bowls, little bowls and receivers. You had big forceps to lift them out. Cat-gut (for stitching wounds) came in large jars – stored in alcohol of some sort. Some came in glass tubes, which you had to break'.*

As well as the main theatres *'we had an emergency theatre, which was in the corridor, between B and C Block, next to casualty'*. It was a complete unit; *'it had a little theatre on the left hand side, an office, a bathroom and anaesthetic room but no recovery room. The windows did not open and there was a chute for dirty laundry. I've sent many a houseman (junior doctor) down to fetch things he'd thrown out'*. It seems that *'nurses preferred to work there'* even though *'it was a funny shift. I went on at 3pm and came off at 12am and was also on call. Matron on the east side lived upstairs in the main block above the entrance. I had a room up there when I was on call. The on-call anaesthetist and on-call doctor were also up there'*. The most common emergencies were *'perforated ulcers, appendicectomies and intestinal obstructions'*. There were always chores to do. *'The far door was where they brought the patients in and we also did things there like making swabs and mending gloves. When we were in emergency theatre and the surgeons had finished with their gloves, they all went into a bucket, washed, put on towels over the radiators to dry, we turned them inside out to dry and if there was hole, we had rubber solution and we used to mend them if there was only a little puncture.'*

Most of these chores disappeared with the introduction of the HSSU (Hospital Sterile Supply Unit) in 1978. This unit was responsible for supplying the wards and theatres with all the instruments; gowns, towels, gloves, swabs and dressings needed for operations and wound care.

After the operation because *'there were no recovery rooms. A nurse came with the patient and a couple of porters. The nurse was there to hold the receiver under the patient's chin in case they vomited'*. On the wards *'we put hot water bottles in the beds of patients for when they came back from theatre. They still used to be under the anaesthetic'*.

Holidays and Off Duty

One nurse told how she *'worked my first year without a holiday because I didn't realise that I could have a holiday after six months. Then after that I had a holiday every six months for a fortnight. You were allowed one month a year. There were no Bank Holidays off'*. What is more *'we had to go to matron and ask for leave and she would tell you when you could be off'*. For those that lived far away this was the only opportunity to go home. *'I used to go home to Newcastle. I went twice a year.'*

'We had a full day off every week' but *'your day off at first, when you were a junior, was a Sunday because no-one wanted a Sunday off. There were no shops open, there was nothing doing on a Sunday'* unless you went to chapel or to church as some did.

It was difficult to get an evening off if you were a junior nurse *'one a week, if you were lucky. It all depended on the senior nurses. There was the sister and staff nurse and the senior nurse, if they had boyfriends, they wanted evenings off'*. Split shifts were normal, *'you had two hours off during the day, which might be 10-12, 2-4, or one 6.15pm finish per week'*. A social life with these hours was difficult even though *'you got off at 4.30pm on a Sunday, if you were on that shift'*.

During the 1930s, *'we had to be in at 10.15pm even with a late pass. You had a key, which you put in the box, so they* (home sister) *knew if they got their key back that you were in'*. But by the 1940s, *'we had to be in by 9pm. Late passes were few and far between, and we were given a key to let ourselves in but home sister was usually waiting behind the door'*. However, *'it was different if you were privileged or a third year nurse'*, or had a room in one of the wooden huts *'which were built during the war, now the social club'* because *'you could get in and out of the window'*.

Nurses made the most of their time off the wards. St Edward's Church was the focal point for the social life of *'the Irish nurses and their friends'* who attended *'the Sunday hops. Several romances flowered during the singing of Faith of our Fathers'*. One former nurse *'used to go to the Methodist Chapel in Selly Oak. That is how I got to know so many people'*. In the Springfields Nurses' Home, *'there was a big recreational hall. We put on a play "Ladies in Retirement"'*. Nurses and doctors regularly put on shows at Christmas, in which they took great delight in making fun of their colleagues. Also *'we had a hospital dance which was held in the dining room of the west side, at the back of K Block. They had a big hall. It was a dance for all the nurses and their partners. Matron stood at the door and shook hands with all the guests and we had to introduce our partners to her. We wore nice dresses and we used to borrow each others' dresses'*. Some nurses *'played a lot of tennis in the courts at the top of Woodlands. There was a silver cup for the Birmingham Hospitals and we won it one year. A shelf was put up on the left hand wall of the dining room for it'*.

Wages

One nurse, who trained from 1947 to 1950 received *'£4.50 when I was a probationer. It became £8 a month when you became a staff nurse'*. This small salary was supplemented. *'You had full board and your laundry was done for you so really you had no expenses other than buying your clothes.'* At that time nurses did appreciate this. *'I suppose we were probably getting £3 to £4 a month. Which wasn't very much but we did get bed and board.'*

Irish Nurses

From the late 1930s, there was a shortage of probationer nurses in Britain and many young women came over from Ireland to train. At Selly Oak Hospital it was not uncommon for Irish nurses to be in the majority. *'There were lots of Irish nurses: out of twenty five in my set, twenty were from Ireland'* and *'out of nineteen members in my preliminary training school at least ten were Irish'*. Once their training was completed many of them stayed, *'most of the wards were staffed by Irish, trained staff'*. One nurse from Ireland started her training in 1947. She had two sisters who also came over to train *'in 1953 and in 1957'*. After completing her midwifery course, she returned to the hospital and took a senior post in the Accident and Emergency Department. She left to become a wife and mother but returned until taking retirement.

These large numbers of Irish nurses made an impact upon the hospital especially on a Sunday. *'Most of the nurses, being Irish, were Roman Catholic. At 9.30am on a Sunday morning, they would all troop down Raddlebarn Road to St. Edward's Church. They had fasted before this and so had breakfast before they returned to their wards at about 11.30am.'* But it was not always possible for all the Irish nurses to go to mass every Sunday as *'somebody had to be in the hospital'*. Matron had a difficult task as she *'couldn't possibly let them all off'*.

Overall impression of working at Selly Oak Hospital
Despite the hard work and discipline, those days were remembered fondly. *'In the nurses' home, we lived together, laughed together and went out together. It was fun and we were friends.'* Another nurse *' loved it. We all had to work very hard and had very long hours'* but *'we knew everybody: the porters, the cleaners, the X-ray staff, the physios, the office staff'*.

The New Out-Patient Department

A nurse, who worked both in the old and new out-patient departments, gave the following description: *'The out-patient department was originally on the ground floor of the main hospital in the old labour wards, close to the old physio and also the sisters' dining room'*. The department was separate from the rest of the hospital. *'We were in the grounds but not attached to anything else. We went in a side entrance.'* The department had been there since 1923.

The new out-patient department was built on the corner of Oak Tree Lane and Raddlebarn Road. The sense of excitement and anticipation can be imagined as the nurses prepared for their new department, which was opened in 1963. Miss Jane, out-patient sister, *'was great, she was there with us. We pushed all sorts of equipment, instruments and things down Raddlebarn Road on a theatre trolley on Good Friday. We opened after the Easter Monday – we went in over the Easter weekend and put stuff in cupboards and set the trolleys up. Miss Jane practically designed the whole place. She went to town on it. She knew what she wanted'*. Dr. Blatchford (Diabetes), Dr. Guest (Neurology), Dr. Phillip (Urology), Dr. Gillian (Cardiology), and Dr. Nussey (Physician) had clinics for their medical patients on the ground floor. The first floor was set up for the surgical teams, led by Mr. Carson, Mr. Sage and Mr. Winstone. When the Eye Department at Exeter Road in Selly Oak closed down in 1966, it was relocated on the first floor. Dr. Henry Giles, a paediatrician, held a Saturday clinic there so that parents could come with their children and not lose any time from their work.

At first, patients had to go to the main hospital for X-rays and blood tests, but it wasn't long before these facilities were provided in the new building. However, the new building was missing two things *'a room for upset relatives and a pram park'*. Eventually, *'a small room just inside the back entrance was designated for a private room'*. The League of Friends furnished and redecorated this small room. It was a haven for distressed patients, often women *'young, middle aged and elderly coming along the corridor from the breast clinic streaming with tears'*.

Outside the back entrance, where the ambulances drew up, was a building for ambulance staff, *'you took your little slips there to order the ambulance'*. This building was later enlarged to house patients' medical records and X-rays required for the out-patient clinics.

M and K Blocks

M Block was built in 1902 to accommodate one hundred female paupers. This huge block looked so big and imposing, that prospective inmates must have felt quite overawed. K Block was built earlier, in 1872, and was one of the original workhouse buildings.

Both blocks housed elderly patients for many years before and after the introduction of the National Health Service.

When geriatric patients were nursed there, the original workhouse function of the M Block could not be disguised. *'The thing about that M Block was that the height of the windows was such that when you were sitting in a chair you couldn't see out.'* Moreover *'the conditions weren't good, you're talking about Victorian buildings, they've stood the test of time but they didn't have all the modern facilities. They tried to paint the walls but you'd still got brick walls'*. It was *'things like that'*, which reminded people *'it was part of the workhouse and patients were there forever'*. In the minds of the elderly the workhouse could not be forgotten.

One nurse remembered that in the late 1970s, *'it took a long time for gerontology to be accepted. It needed to blend into general medicine and then it was decided that everyone over sixty five would be admitted to a geriatric ward. It took quite a lot of years for the hospital to be amalgamated as one. At one time the west side was under the supervision of West Heath and Moseley Hall Hospitals'*. West Heath Hospital was originally opened as King's Norton Infectious Diseases Hospital in 1889. In 1965, the Sheldon Unit, at West Heath Hospital, was opened for geriatric care and by 1980 it was wholly used for the care of elderly people. Moseley Hall, a gift from the Cadbury family in 1948, was used for acute child cases and later became a hospital for the elderly and chronic sick.

Other memories about the workhouse were, *'my sister reminded me, although she doesn't actually remember it herself, that my mother told her that when the old were admitted to the infirmary, I'm talking about when it was still the workhouse, although it was called the infirmary in those days, the inmates used to wear grey cloaks'*. Another person recalled that, *'mum had a friend who worked in the workhouse part. As a child mum would take us and point out where the vagrants were bedded. The place hasn't changed much since I was a child'*.

Over the years many measures were taken to improve the facilities, one such being the installation of a wireless (radio) service. It was reported in the Birmingham Gazette of 31st May 1927 that this was 'for the benefit of the aged and infirm inmates' and 'was accompanied by scenes which would have delighted the thousands of subscribers to the Birmingham Gazette Hospital Wireless Fund'. By the 1980s, matters had improved considerably and one lady remembered *'visiting on M3 a couple of times within the last twenty years and then they were clean, pleasant light wards. Those sort of places had high ceilings and lots of light because it was considered healthy, which it was'*. But there was no getting away from the workhouse association. Another lady recounted how *'my mother lived to be ninety and she died at Selly Oak on M Block. I didn't dare tell her and she was in for six months. She used to say to me "where exactly am I?" So I used to avoid this question by looking through the window and saying "I can see St. Mary's Church". There was no way I could tell her exactly where she was. She would have said "You've put me in the workhouse"'*. There was no getting away from *'it was the infirmary and the old people were there'* and being admitted to the geriatric wards was final, *'mum died in the infirmary'*. Even into the late 1990s the idea of being admitted into Selly Oak Hospital was for elderly patients a real fear. *'You'll find any old person, and my friend's aunt is 108, any one of her age or my mother's age regarded it as the workhouse, never anything except the workhouse, not the hospital.'* But it may also have been that old people remembered *'the stigma and the fact you got separated from your husband. It was a real dread, a real fear'*. Elderly patients must have been very concerned when they were transferred from the hospital across to the workhouse side, *'because we used to send patients from accident and emergency, and in those days we didn't have an ambulance, and we used to put a mackintosh over the trolley when patients were transferred over to the chronic side'*. This practice continued into the 1960s when *'they were still wheeling patients across on trolleys to the infirmary in my time at Selly Oak Hospital'*.

K Block also had beds for the chronic sick. One person tells how *'K Block had double doors at the front with wards on either side made up of small rooms and a balcony above inside the building. Patients lived upstairs and downstairs and worked in the hospital'*. In the late 1940s, *'when I started the kitchen was in K Block for the west side, there was a dining hall at the back of K Block for the nursing staff. I was chef in the kitchen there'*.

The dining hall was used during the 1940s and 1960s for various staff parties. A senior nurse, who came over from Ireland to train at Selly Oak Hospital and remained to become a ward sister and then an assistant matron, organised many *'parties for the cleaners, their husbands, the porters and their wives on the two Saturdays preceding Christmas'*. There were so many cleaners and porters that it was necessary to have two parties. 'Admission was by tickets collected with the weekly wages. The hall was decorated with paper chains. Tables were placed around the edge of the wooden floor. People would arrive at about 6pm with their own glasses and bottles of beer and sherry. A blind eye was turned to alcoholic refreshment and people did not get drunk. There wasn't enough for that. The catering officer produced colossal amounts of food; meat sandwiches with ham, tongue or spam and perhaps a bit of lettuce and sandwich cakes filled with jam or icing. The women would dress up in skirts and blouses and the men in their best suits. There was a band, although not much dancing was done, except for the occasional old fashioned waltz or Gay Gordons or Veleta. At the end we sang "Auld Lang Syne". The night porters cleared up after the festivities. There was usually food left over and the bags carried by the women were never empty when they went home.'

A more comprehensive description provides further information about the block in the 1960s and early 70s. 'There were geriatric wards: K1 (male) and K2 (female) on the ground floor and K3 and K4 upstairs which were possibly mixed wards. Some patients, who didn't go to Blackwell to convalesce, were moved there post surgery. There were patients in nooks and crannies everywhere. It was dark and "Dickensian". Turn a corner and there would be three or four elderly patients. There were open gutters running down the ward. I think they were the original drains from the workhouse days.' A few years later 'all the patients were moved out' and 'the poor old people were pushed in wheelchairs from K Block to M Block, with carrier bags containing all they possessed. Some had been there for years, as many as thirteen or fourteen, and didn't live long after the move'.

K Block was refurbished and in 1975 the physiotherapy and occupational therapy departments were opened there.

Keeping the Hospital Clean
Elbow Grease and Housemaid's Knee

Keeping hospitals clean, before the days of electric vacuum cleaners and floor polishers, called for physical stamina and determination. Domestic and nursing staff worked tirelessly to make sure that hospitals were spotless. Strong smelling disinfectants gave hospitals a distinctive and pervasive smell which seemed to combine the elements of cleanliness, efficiency and apprehension depending upon whether you were a member of staff or a patient. The large wards connected by a maze of long, echoing corridors made hospitals daunting places and Selly Oak Hospital was no exception.

The main ground floor corridor was a busy, bustling place with people constantly going to and fro. Scrubbing the length of this corridor was a daily chore for one woman, who scoured it with a large wooden scrubbing brush and used a cake of red carbolic soap to get a good lather, which was then rinsed off with a cloth and large amounts of water. What an interminable task it must have seemed; the corridor ran the length of the hospital from the pharmacy at one end, past the ward blocks, dining room, kitchens and X-ray department to the operating theatres at the far end. She started at 8 am and finished at midday, scrubbing one side of the corridor until she reached the top when she turned round and scrubbed the other half. Most of those passing by were careful not to step on the wet, newly washed floor, although occasionally a few did, as one former nurse put it, *'transgress'*. Once the scrubbing was over the cleaner could look forward to repeating the same job the next day and the next. Imagine her red, chapped, sore hands: no rubber gloves for such tasks in those days, and her aching back, knees, shoulders and elbows. No wonder such vigorous, manual cleaning was described as 'elbow grease' and that 'housemaid's knee' was a common rheumatic complaint. Although the cleaner given this task was provided with a kneeling pad, it would not have given her aching knees much relief. A thick flannel apron protected her clothes from the wetness of such a sloppy job. One woman, who undertook this task regularly, is reported as being able to recognize the doctors by their feet. Down on her hands and knees and not even lifting her head she would say *'Morning Mr. Gore, morning Mr. Parsons'*. When asked how she knew them, she replied *'Cos, Mr. Gore's heels are always worn down, and Mr. Parsons' shoes are always polished'*. Eventually this particular lady *'rose to a mop and bucket'*.

On the wards, domestic and nursing staff shared the cleaning. It was quite normal for the ward sister to run her finger over surfaces and ledges to check that they had been dusted. Each ward had two cleaners. In the morning they washed floors, cleaned sinks and toilets and in the evening they had to wash woodwork, polish window brasses and wooden surfaces and then serve and clear away the patients' suppers. One former patient compared the 'good old days' with today. *'Well I've been in recently and if Matron saw all of this now she'd go mad. The ward cleaners had to work very hard and they were everlasting coming around mopping and cleaning. Nowadays the cleaner puts the mop on a stick, puts it in the bucket, swishes it around and then she goes all round the bed in two seconds and under the bed. She'll do four beds with one mop.'* Visitors also noticed: *'My sister-in-law said. "Just look under that bed. Fluff like a carpet." She had worked in the hospital during the War and said "If we'd have done that. People just don't know how to clean".'*

At least once a day the junior nurses tidied and damp dusted the patients' lockers. Sometimes used, damp, tea leaves were scattered over the wooden floors and were then swept up along with the dust and fluff from under the beds. The cleaners then used 'bumpers', large felt pads fixed to stout broom handles, to buff the floors up to a good shine. Once a week the high dusting was done using a long handled soft brush to make sure neither dust nor spiders' webs were lurking in the corners above the doors and lights. Each morning before the ward sister came on duty at eight o'clock, sheets and blankets were stripped from the beds which were then made up with fresh linen. The windows were opened to air the ward and the wheels at the ends of the beds were arranged to point in the same direction. Night nurses were often given the job of removing hair and fluff from the wheels of trolleys and screens and then oiling them.

Cleaning never stopped and it could be a means of escape. Many nurses remembered using the sluice room as a refuge, especially in the early days of their training. Cleaning bedpans, urinals and vomit bowls was often preferable to being on the open ward under the stern gaze of sister or one of the consultants. A lot of satisfaction could be gained from scrubbing walls and floors and tidying away dirty linen before the next bedpan round.

The Maids

Maids were an integral part of hospital life until the late 1960s. There was a distinction between those that served and those that cleaned; *'they were maids not cleaners, they were marvellous, they looked after us so well'*.

The maids wore a uniform *'they had a striped dress, blue and white'* and *'the senior ones wore a black dress with a little apron and a cap'*. This was when they waited on the medical and nursing staff in their individual dining rooms *'to serve dinner'*. The maids too, *' had their own dining room'*. One maid had a different task from her colleagues. *'Miss Brown had a little dog that the maid, who lived in the Matron's house, walked around the grounds.'* It seems that she lived over on the west side. *'The majority of the maids were resident. They lived up there, upstairs above the hospital entrance.'* This was also where the on-call doctors and nurses lived. One nurse, who worked in the emergency theatre, had fond memories of the maids. *'Gladys was from Wales. She used to put coal on my fire before she went to bed and stoked it up so that it was nice and warm, when I went to bed at twelve.'* Some maids were local women who *'finished and went home. There was Doris, Winnie and Gladys. Dear old Doris was local she had a Birmingham accent. They were all lovely'*.

The front of Selly Oak Hospital circa 1970s.
At one time, on-call doctors and nurses, and the maids lived in the upper rooms above the entrance. (Photograph courtesy Joan Teasedale and Medical Illustration – University Hospitals Birmingham NHS Foundation Trust)

The Porters

Porters provided a service throughout the day and night and were important for the smooth running of the hospital. They wore uniform, *'you had the black trousers, white shirt, black tie. They provided everything. If you didn't get a uniform, you were put on another job until you got one'.*

Their main job was looking after hospital security. One porter, who started work at Selly Oak Hospital in 1947, remembered that *'security was wonderful. When I first started there were a hundred and twenty one porters. The railings were all the way round and there were two gates and a lodge. I worked on the lodge and we used to book every ambulance in'.* They also checked all visitors and members of staff in. *'Everyone was known, they had to clock in and out.'* This reflected the role of the workhouse porters, who used to check goods and people in and out of the West Lodge.

Main Entrance to Selly Oak Hospital 1970s. The porters' lodge was demolished and it was made open-plan in the 1950s. (Photograph courtesy Joan Teasedale and Medical Illustration – University Hospitals Birmingham NHS Foundation Trust)

There were chief porters, deputy porters, day porters and night porters. *'First you started as a lodge porter and then you became a senior porter.'* Large departments such as X-ray, out-patients, theatres and casualty had their own specific porters. Porters were responsible for taking patients around the hospital in wheelchairs and on trolleys, fetching and carrying medical notes and equipment, moving hospital food trolleys and taking bodies to the mortuary. Some jobs were not pleasant, *'they used to have a dustbin on two wheels and they used to have to do all the dressings and the smell was dreadful. The west side porters used to do the dressings'*.

When the porters' lodge was demolished and *'they decided it should be open plan'*, sometime in the 1950s, the porters were given a desk in the main hospital. From there they were able to coordinate their duties throughout the hospital. The porters knew everybody and *'it was "Mr. Porter, Sir, can you help me? Thank you very much"'*. The same porter was fulsome in his praise of Selly Oak Hospital. *'It was a great place to work and I couldn't say anything bad about it. It brings tears to my eyes sometimes, when I think how good Selly Oak was and the people. They always treated me wonderfully.'*

The Social Club and Sports Field

The wooden hut outside the Woodlands Nurses' Home was erected during World War II to provide extra accommodation for nurses. It eventually became home to the social club and was open during lunch hours and in the evenings. One woman remembered her mother who was a member of the domestic staff having *'a good social life at Selly Oak Hospital through the social club. The social club organised trips to Stratford, the theatres in London, coach trips and weekends away and a dinner and dance at the Chateau Impney hotel'*.

Up until the 1990s, it was a popular venue for staff parties, especially around Christmas time. It was not unknown for some members of staff to meet there for a quick half pint during their lunch hour. In the summer months a hospital cricket team played home games, on the pitch outside the social club. It was a lovely setting and cheering the team on was a very relaxing way of spending a summer evening. *'There used to be a lovely cricket pavilion by the cricket pitch on the other side where the staff flats are now.'* There were also several tennis courts outside the Woodlands and during the 1920s, 30s and 40s, teams used to compete for a hospitals' cup. Tennis was also played on the courts at the back of the hospital where S Block was erected.

The social life at Selly Oak Hospital was extremely good and there was a tremendous sense of being part of *'a little village on its own. Every one knew everyone else and in a way it seemed like a great big family'*.

Smokey Joe's

Another place where the sense of belonging was apparent was Smokey Joe's, a pre-fabricated building situated close to the main entrance. There was no ban on smoking which was generally accepted inside canteens and restaurants until the late 1990s – hence the name. As a retired porter described it, *'Smokey Joe's was originally put up as a canteen, for everybody, that was one of the good things about it. We all used to mix in there everybody used to come in. It was very nice and the public was let in'*. Around it were gardens *'laid out with summertime plants and bushes, somebody presented a lot of roses'*.

Smokey Joe's was popular with all members of staff and many recalled it with fond memories. The meals were good, with lots of chips and wonderful steamed puddings and custard, served by cheerful, chatty women. Elderly local people often went there for lunch as they could enjoy an inexpensive, good meal in a jolly atmosphere with lots of company. *'I used to like going into Smokey Joe's. They used to have on a Friday, cheese pie made with potato. It was absolutely delicious. They were really nice people in there.'*

It was a sad day when the building burnt down, sometime in the late 1980s. It was never replaced.

The Harry Payne Pavilion

Another prefabricated building was the Harry Payne Pavilion erected behind the casual wards. The Payne family, the '*shoe people*', gave it to the hospital for the use of the nurses. It was eventually taken over for offices much to the annoyance of the nursing staff. '*One of the staff nurses on surgery wrote to the Payne family and told them what had happened. They did kick up a fuss but nothing changed.*' During the 1990s this building was the print room. There were very pleasant gardens to the front of it laid out with mature shrubs and trees.

Green Spaces and Car Parks

Some of the many green spaces on the hospital site were originally airing or exercise yards for the workhouse inmates as can be seen on the ordnance survey map of 1884 which show the walls that separated the different classes of paupers. During that time other areas would have been given over for vegetable growing and the keeping of pigs and poultry. In later years these became gardens, open green spaces and car parks.

Until the 1960s or 70s, *'there was a large garden, with big greenhouses, on the site of the large car park'*. One former ward sister remembered *'quite a few gardeners who used to send flowers up to Matron'*. She herself *'would pick flowers for her ward, which was for men, who rarely had flowers'*. A retired porter recalled, *'The head gardener had a wonderful crew. He used to say, "You can have anything you want but please make sure no-one knows about it". Starting from the back of E Block the greenhouses ran along there right up to the canal. They grew vegetables in the wartime, as far as I know. But they grew flowers by the thousand and they brought them into the hospital. They were put out of the wards at night. It was a marvellous garden, where the car parks are now'*.

The Laundry

There was a laundry on the edge of the gardens close by E Block. *'The laundry burnt down before the 80s. The woman in charge ruled it with a rod of iron. Those girls worked like slaves in there. They wore wellingtons'*. Previously, in the workhouse days, it was the inmates who worked in the laundry and it seems that the strict working conditions of that time prevailed long into the 20th century. Records for the 1920s show that several fourteen and a half year old girls were employed as laundry pupils for ten shillings a week and that some of them received a certificate after four years.

This building was converted into a physiotherapy block in 1951 and demolished in the 1980s.

Christmas

Christmas in hospital was a very special time. It was rare for nursing staff to get time off over the Christmas period whatever their position in the hierarchy. Many of the young probationers were a long way from their homes and so much planning went into the celebrations at the hospital. If the nurses did by any chance get the time off *'you didn't want to come home at Christmas because it was fantastic and the atmosphere was wonderful'*.

Each ward had a Christmas tree and *'the wards were decorated by the nurses'*. Even local stores were involved and as one nurse remembered *'Rackhams used to supply decorations. There was always a competition as to who had the best decorated ward'*. Nurses used their imaginations and any materials they had to hand such as cotton wool or gauze to make the place look festive. In 1953, Ward B2 used an axe and rope, loaned by Colonel John Hunt, the leader of the successful expedition to Mount Everest earlier the same year, as the centre piece for their wintery Christmas display.

Nurses enjoyed the temporary relaxation in discipline. *'We went round the wards and did a pantomime. Somebody pushed a piano around. We used a spinal carriage; they were long, basketwork things that they used to push patients outside. Everything was piled up on one of those and we would go to the next ward. I don't know if the*

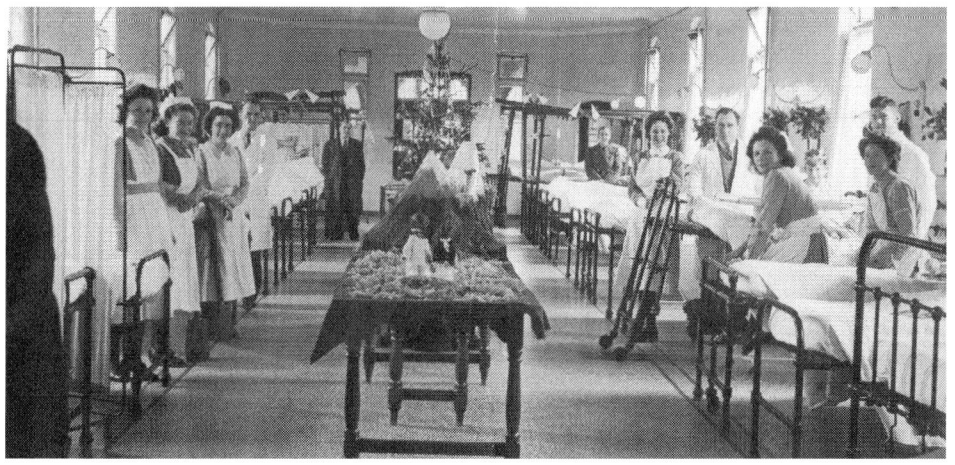

Christmas on Ward B2 1947. (Photograph courtesy Joan Teasedale)

patients enjoyed it, but we found it funny.' The ward sisters had special funds to buy small presents for their patients and nurses. In 1936, a young girl who was the only child occupant of a ward on K Block was given *'a great big cracker by the nurses'*. During the afternoon another child was admitted and she was told that she *'had to share her cracker'*. She remembered not being too happy about that!

On Christmas Eve nurses traditionally toured the wards, singing carols *'with their cloaks turned inside out, they were black with red inside, and they carried lanterns. The Police Choir used to come'* and local church choirs sang carols for *'the old people'* on K Block.

In 1961 the nurses toured the wards on the east side to sing carols while on the west side a carol party was held and also a service on Ward F for the children and their parents. The Lord Mayor and Lady Mayoress of Birmingham visited the hospital and were entertained to lunch in Springfields Nurses' Home. Over this same Christmas period the catering staff prepared and cooked eighty-six turkeys amounting to over half a ton in weight. These were not only for patients but also for the staff Christmas Dinners, *'which were the usual riotous affairs'*. A former nurse remembered *'there was always a Christmas dance for the staff that was held at Springfields'* and in 1969, two dances were held there for the nurses as well as two staff socials *'when there was much letting down of hair'*. To crown all these festivities there was also, in that year, an annual Christmas staff dance in the Undergraduates' Union at Birmingham University.

During the 1990s, the rheumatology consultants used to invite severely disabled patients who lived alone to spend Christmas on Ward E2 as in-patients. It was one way to make sure that these vulnerable people would enjoy the festive spirit and receive care at a time when this was not necessarily available in their own homes. On Christmas Day *'all the doctors and surgeons came round and visited their various wards'*. Up until the late 1990s, most consultant doctors and surgeons came to their wards to carve the turkey at lunchtime. Some consultants would wear quirky Christmas hats and aprons to amuse the patients and nurses. With the introduction of plated meals there was no longer a need to carve the turkey and yet many consultants continued to visit their wards to 'do the rounds' of their patients and enter into the Christmas spirit. Patients were served the traditional Christmas meal of roast turkey and stuffing, pudding and mince pies. Nursing and medical staff had cold buffet food on Christmas and Boxing Days so that some of the catering staff could have time off with their families.

This was a happy time and former members of staff have very fond memories. *'At Christmas time you were invited to the X-ray department for sherry with the trained staff and the sisters from the various departments.'*

The Visit of Princess Elizabeth and the Duke of Edinburgh 1949

A letter from the Chairman of Group No. 25, Birmingham (Selly Oak) Hospital Management Committee, Alderman Albert Bradbeer, to all members of staff after the visit of Princess Elizabeth and the Duke of Edinburgh on 10th May 1949 relayed the 'sincere thanks and deep appreciation' of the Royal couple. The Lord Mayor also offered his congratulations on the excellent arrangements that were made, 'the whole place looked so nice and fresh and their Royal Highnesses were able to see not only a representative selection of patients, but what I feel is equally important, to have an opportunity of meeting and being seen by your hard worked staff'. One member of staff stood just inside the big window by the main entrance, very close to Princess Elizabeth, she remembered that the Princess '*looked lovely*'.

The young couple spent an hour and a half at the hospital, during which time they met members of the Hospital Management Committee and a representative selection of members of staff: Mr. Kelman (Medical Superintendent), Miss Poole (Matron of the east side), Miss E.V. Wheeler (Matron of the west side), several nurses of different ranks and members of the domestic and portering services.

The Royal Wedding in November 1947 had been a cause for much rejoicing and brought a touch of fairy tale magic and hope to the war weary British public, still recovering from the trauma of the conflict with Nazi Germany. Photographs show staff and dignitaries awaiting the arrival of the young couple outside the main entrance to the hospital, and the Princess and her tall husband being escorted by her ladies in waiting, nursing and medical staff through a ward, where patients lay in bed with their legs in plaster.

Some members of staff were invited to the Recreation Hall at Springfields, '*where tea will be taken with Their Royal Highnesses*'. One former nurse remembered, '*I was chosen to be in the hall. They sat at the top table and we had a full view. Unfortunately we never had any photographs*'. Another nurse '*was invited to tea when Princess Elizabeth came. We had sandwiches and little cakes. All the dignitaries sat around and the Royal couple had their tea, then smiled at everybody*

Princess Elizabeth and the Duke of Edinburgh visiting Ward B2. (Photograph courtesy Medical Illustration – University Hospitals Birmingham NHS Foundation Trust)

and went out. They spoke to one or two, but not to us lowly beings'. The same nurse recalled 'my grandmother was so proud that they wheeled her to sit outside the Nurses' Home to see me'.

The Friends of Selly Oak Hospital

It was common for most hospitals to be supported by voluntary groups that raised sums of money for the benefit of patients and staff, and Selly Oak Hospital was no exception. The 'Friends Association', also known as the 'League of Friends' was formed in 1953, originally as a 'Personal Service' assisting on wards with 'the feeding of patients or in Casualty and in visiting patients without relatives or friends'.

The main purpose of the 'Friends' however, was to 'supplement the resources of the Hospital Management Committee'. For many years the President was Mrs. Laurence Cadbury and the Assistant Secretary was Mrs. Jenny Eley, who trained at Selly Oak Hospital in the 1930s. By 1975 the 'Friends' had raised £30,000 in funds and provided television sets and radios for the older patients besides decorating and furnishing the day rooms 'as now geriatric patients do not lie in bed all day and acute patients get up much quicker than in the past'. One former hospital clerk recalled that, *'they collected enough money to put a lift in to take the patients up from K Block to K2 and K3'* which would have been really useful for the staff and elderly patients of K Block. The 'Friends' also provided toys and books for the children, equipment for the Nursing School, a table tennis table for the nurses, and an altar rail and baptismal bowl for the Chapel.

Money was raised in many ways. One lady remembered, *'My dad used to walk his legs off collecting stuff and he used to make quite a lot of money, hundreds in aid of the "Friends" of the hospital'*. Local people and staff would make or donate items to sell at the hospital bazaar and fete, an event that was held every summer, until the late 1980s, on the cricket field outside the Woodlands Nurses' Home.

Chapter 8

Conclusion

It was the end of an era when the doors of Selly Oak Hospital were finally closed to patients and services were transferred to the new Queen Elizabeth Hospital. Innumerable people had passed through those doors, workhouse inmates, patients, visitors, and staff. The buildings had stood the test of time and been witness to many scenes of drama. In the early workhouse days many of those scenes were, no doubt, ones which are probably best forgotten. At the time the treatment meted out to paupers was questionable even by the standards of the day. Today they would be unacceptable. However, we cannot realistically judge history from the benefit of our situation, wrapped as we are in the blanket of the Welfare State. In a hundred years time our descendants might well have a different view of matters that we find acceptable today.

Selly Oak Hospital was a venerable institution with memories, not just for members of staff, but also for patients and local residents. It was part of the local landscape for nearly a century and a half. As a Victorian establishment it provided care for the destitute. The opening of the Infirmary in 1897 saw the beginning of a proud tradition: the provision of healthcare to thousands of people and the training of doctors, nurses and paramedical staff. The pattern of health care has changed radically and the reorganisation of hospitals within the Birmingham area has reflected this change with the subsequent closures of several of them. Selly Oak Hospital survived but ultimately the age and the variety and number of buildings meant that it was no longer a viable site for the provision of modern day health care.

So today, in 2015, we find the site enclosed by security fencing. Demolition has already started on some of the buildings and the whole area is due to be cleared by the end of 2015. It is amazing that an institution that has seen so much activity over the past one hundred and forty years will be eradicated in such a short space of time and that the hospital will eventually be forgotten except in the memories of those whose lives it has touched. Maybe this book will help preserve some tangible reminder of Selly Oak Hospital and its important role in the history of Birmingham.

Timeline

1834 The Poor Law Amendment Act.
1836 King's Norton Poor Law Union formed.
1869 Land purchased at Raddlebarn Road, Selly Oak by the Board of Guardians.
1872 King's Norton Union Workhouse opened.
1878 Erection of Casual Wards for Males and the Pump House.
1882 Erection of Infectious Hospital and Boundary Wall.
1887 Shenley Fields Cottage Homes opened.
1893 Purchase of land adjoining the Workhouse.
1894 The Workhouse had 421 inmates – there was only provision for 350.
1895 Foundation stone laid for the new Workhouse Infirmary.
1897 King's Norton Poor Law Union Workhouse Infirmary was opened in May.
1901 Death of Queen Victoria.
1902 Erection of M Block, West Lodge, L Block and Casual Wards on Oaktree Lane.
1905 Monyhull Hall purchased by Aston, Birmingham and King's Norton Unions.
1908 A and D Blocks added to the Infirmary. Woodlands Nurses' Home built.
1908 Old Age Pensions Act.
1911 National Insurance Act.
1911 King's Norton Urban District became part of the Birmingham metropolis.
1912 King's Norton Union and Aston Union joined Birmingham Union.
1912 Workhouse renamed Birmingham Union Workhouse. (Selly Oak Infirmary and Selly Oak Hospital)
1914-1918 World War I.
1915 National Registration Act. (Births, Deaths and Marriages)
1923 First Physiotherapy, Out-Patient and X-ray Departments. Pathology service.
1925 Rating and Valuation Act.
1927 Extension the Woodlands Nurses' Home, new kitchens and dining room.
1928 New operating theatres.
1929 Extension to Woodlands Nurses' Home.
1929 Local Government Act.
1930 End of the Poor Law.

Timeline

1930	Selly Oak Hospital became a municipal hospital under the jurisdiction of Birmingham City Council.
1934	Biochemistry and Pathology laboratory opened.
1937	Lady Almoner appointed.
1938	Queen Elizabeth Hospital, Edgbaston opened.
1939-1945	World War II.
1942	Amy Bodley School of Nursing opened.
1946	National Health Service Act.
1947	Springfield Nurses' Home opened.
1948	**Implementation of NHS Act.**
1948	Selly Oak Hospital administered by Birmingham Regional Hospital Board.
1948	National Assistance Act.
1949	Visit of HRH Princess Elizabeth and the Duke of Edinburgh.
1951	Veitch Physiotherapy Department opened.
1953	West and East Sides become one hospital.
1954	Hospital Chapel dedicated.
1962	New Operating Theatres.
1963	New Out-Patient Department opened in Oak Tree Lane.
1968	Coronary Care Unit opened.
1969	Maternity services transferred to the Queen Elizabeth Hospital.
1975	Department of Gerontology opened in the Hayward Building.
1975	Physiotherapy and Occupational Therapy Departments opened in K Block.
1978	S Block opened.
1991	Department of Rheumatology opened in E Block.
1991	South and Central Birmingham Health Districts are merged.
1995	Accident Hospital closed.
1995	New Accident and Emergency Department and Intensive Care Unit opened.
1996	General Hospital closed.
1997	University Hospital Birmingham National Health Service Trust Queen Elizabeth and Selly Oak Hospital become University Hospital, Birmingham.
2001	The Royal Centre for Defence Medicine opened in K Block.
2006	Birmingham University Hospital National Health Service Foundation Trust.
2010	A and E service transferred to the new Queen Elizabeth Hospital from Selly Oak Hospital.
2012	All health services transferred from Selly Oak Hospital.
2012	Closure of the hospital.

Sources

Introduction

Cook K. (1972) Paper on the History of Selly Oak Hospital; Birmingham City Archives.

Higginbotham Peter, (2007 reprint 2009) Workhouses of The Midlands; The History Press, Stroud, Gloucestershire.

Land Neville (1998) Victorian Workhouse. A Study of the Bromsgrove Union Workhouse 1836-1901; Brewin Books, Studley, Warwickshire.

Longmate N. (2003) Whipped to Death, Chapter 1 in The Workhouse; Pimlico, London.

May Trevor (2003) The Victorian Workhouse, Shire Publications; Princes Risborough, Buckinghamshire.

National Trust (2002) The Workhouse Southwell; National Trust (Enterprises) Ltd., London.

Chapter 1: King's Norton Poor Law Union

Carter C.A. (1911) The Guardians of the Poor in Birmingham Institutions, Edited by J.H. Muirhead; Cornish Brothers, Birmingham.

Coley A.H. (1911) The Council Schools in Birmingham Institutions, Edited by J.H. Muirhead; Cornish Brothers, Birmingham.

Dowling G., Giles B., Hayfield C. (1987) Selly Oak Past and Present. A Photographic Survey of a Birmingham Suburb; Department of Geography, University of Birmingham.

Hutchings Deborah (1998) Monyhull 1908-1998 A History of Caring; Brewin Books, Studley, Warwickshire.

Lloyd J.H. (1911) The Hospitals in Birmingham Institutions, Edited by J.H. Muirhead; Cornish Brothers, Birmingham.

Longmate N. (2003) Mr. Chadwick's Cold Bath, Chapter 5 in The Workhouse; Pimlico, London.

Longmate N. (2003) The End of the Workhouse, Chapter 23 in The Workhouse; Pimlico, London.

Official Handbook King's Norton Union 1902-3; Birmingham City Archives.

Official Handbook King's Norton Union 1906-7; Birmingham City Archives.

Plumley J. (1992) The Children's Home Village; Shenley Fields Cottage Homes; Brewin Books, Studley, Warwickshire.

Chapter 2: King's Norton Union Workhouse
Bird Vivian (1970) Coals by Canal, Chapter IV; in Portrait of Birmingham; Robert Hale, London.
Building News (1902) 18th July; page 73. Birmingham Central Library.
Census 1881; www.national archives.gov.uk/census.
Harrison J.F. (1967) No Trumpets at King's Norton in Historical Sketches of the West Midlands: the West Midlands Physicians' Society; Warwickshire Publishing Co. Ltd., Birmingham.
Kelly's Directory of Birmingham 1884.
Kelly's Directory of Worcestershire 1880.
King's Norton Union Contract (1901) for the Erection of new Receiving Ward, Stores and offices, Pavilion and Other Buildings at the Workhouse, Selly Oak; Birmingham City Archives.
Morrison Kathryn (1996) Report to The Royal Commission on the Historical Monuments of England. West Midlands, Birmingham. Kings Norton Workhouse, Selly Oak. NBR NO: 100913. NGR: SP 045 821.
Official Handbook King's Norton Union 1902-3; Birmingham City Archives.
Official Handbook King's Norton Union 1906-7; Birmingham City Archives.
Ordnance Survey Map (1884) Surveyed (1882); Ordnance Survey Office, Southampton.
Ordnance Survey Map (1904) Second Edition; Ordnance Survey Office, Southampton.

Chapter 3: Life in the Workhouse
Census 1881; www.national archives.gov.uk/census.
Census 1901; www.national archives.gov.uk/census.
Higginbotham P. (2007) The Workhouse, Staff and Administration www.workhouses.org.uk.
Kelly's Directory of Birmingham 1900.
King's Norton Union (2nd July, 1900) Provisions and Consumption Accounts; Birmingham City Archives.
Local Government Board Letters to and from King's Norton Union 1900-1901; Birmingham City Archives.
Longmate N. (2003) The Pauper Palace, Chapter 7 in The Workhouse; Pimlico, London.
Longmate N. (2003) Master and Matron, Chapter 8 in The Workhouse; Pimlico, London.
Longmate N. (2003) Aged Inmates of Respectable Character, Chapter 11 in The Workhouse; Pimlico, London.
Longmate N. (2003) Death in the Workhouse Chapter 12 in The Workhouse; Pimlico, London.
May Trevor (2003) Staffing the Workhouse in The Victorian Workhouse; Shire Publications Ltd., Princes Risborough, Buckinghamshire.

Chapter 4: The Casual (Vagrants') Wards

Davies W.H. (1908) (Reprint 1964) The Autobiography of a Super Tramp; Jonathan Cape, London.

Digby A (1978) Pauper Palaces; Routledge and Kegan Paul, London.

Official Handbook King's Norton Union 1902-3; Birmingham City Archives.

Official Handbook King's Norton Union 1906-7; Birmingham City Archives.

King's Norton Union (1901) Register of Admission and Discharge of Casual Paupers; Birmingham City Archives.

Longmate N. (2003) Tramps and Vagrants, Chapter 19 in The Workhouse; Pimlico, London.

Morrison Kathryn (1999) Poor Law Buildings for Vagrants and the 'Houseless Poor', Chapter 10 in The Workhouse: A Study of Poor Law buildings in England; English Heritage, Swindon.

Chapter 5: King's Norton Union Workhouse Infirmary

Birmingham Union (1920) Statement of Accounts for the Seven Years ended 31st March, 1919; Birmingham City Archives.

British Journal (January 10th, 1914) Poor Law Institutions (Nursing) Order 1913.

British Medical Journal (July 22nd, 1944) Book Review of 'The Hospital Almoner' by Dorothy Manchee; Balliere, Tindall and Cox, London.

British Journal of Nursing (January 1952) The Opening of the Veitch Physiotherapy and Dental Department, Selly Oak Hospital, Birmingham.

Census (1901); www.nationalarchives.gov.uk/census.

Harrison J.F. (1967) No Trumpets at King's Norton in Historical Sketches of the West Midlands: the West Midlands Physicians' Society. Warwickshire Publishing Co. Ltd., Birmingham.

King's Norton Union 1897-1906 Register of Nurses and Servants at the Workhouse Infirmary; Birmingham City Archives.

King's Norton Union Infirmary – Order of the Local Government Board (Regulations, Duties, Clothes and Diet 1900); Birmingham City Archives.

King's Norton Union Infirmary – Order of the Local Government Board (1900) Regulations for the Appointment and Government of the Workhouse of that Union; Birmingham City Archives.

King's Norton Union (1902) Report of Departmental Committee into the Nursing of the Sick Poor in Workhouses; Birmingham City Archives.

Longmate N. (2003) The Lame and the Blind, Chapter 16 in The Workhouse; Pimlico, London.

Morrison Kathryn (1999) The Workhouse after 1914, Chapter 11 in The Workhouse: A Study of Poor Law buildings in England; English Heritage, Swindon.

Nussey A.M. (1967) F.W. Ellis in Historical Sketches of the West Midlands: the West Midlands Physicians' Society; Warwickshire Publishing Co. Ltd., Birmingham.

Phelps A. Lieut-General (1900) The Selly Oak Workhouse Infirmary; A Strange Tale of Stifled Discussion. Furtive Mismanagement, and Scandalous Waste; The Midland Educational Company Limited, Birmingham.

Sources

Chapter 6: Selly Oak Hospital

BBC WW2 People's War 1939-1945. www.bbc.co.uk/history/www2peoples war.

Birmingham Health Authority, South Birmingham Health District, Selly Oak Hospital, (1978) Commemorative Menu for 'The Opening of S Block'; Birmingham City Archives.

Birmingham Regional Hospital Board 1947-1966 (A Comprehensive Review); Arthur Thompson House, 146-150 Hagley Road, Edgbaston, Birmingham.

Birmingham Regional Hospital Board, Birmingham (Selly Oak Hospital Management Committee) (1963) Programme for the Opening of the New Out-Patient Department of Selly Oak Hospital; Birmingham City Archives.

Journal of British Geriatric Society (March 2005) South Birmingham: two trusts in one service. News BGS 27.

Nagle R.E. (c 1968) Coronary Care Unit – Selly Oak Hospital, Research Report; Birmingham City Archives.

NHS Hospital Plan for England and Wales 1962, Birmingham Regions 206-213.

McLaughlin N. (c 1960's) The New Theatres; Birmingham City Archives.

Public Monument and Sculpture Association. www.pmsa.cch.kcl.ac.uk

RCN Rheumatology Nursing Forum, Newsletter (1991) Issue 6. The Rheumatology Unit at Selly Oak Hospital.

Selly Oak Hospital, Birmingham. Nurse Training School. Booklet 1957; Birmingham City Archives.

Selly Oak Hospital Medical Staff Committee Meeting. Notes on a meeting with the Dean of the Medical School at Birmingham University 1969; Birmingham City Archives.

Selly Oak Hospital Staff Journal (Spring 1962) Vol 1. No.1; Birmingham City Archives.

Royal Centre for Defence Medicine. University Hospitals Birmingham NHS Foundation Trust. www.uhb.nhs.uk.

Chapter 7: Memories of Selly Oak Hospital

Birmingham (Selly Oak) Hospital Management Committee Group 25 (1962) Notes for the Guidance of In-Patients; Birmingham City Archives.

Birmingham Regional Hospital Board, Birmingham (Selly Oak) Hospital Management Committee (1963), Programme for the Opening of the New Out-Patient Department; Birmingham City Archives.

Friends of Selly Oak Hospital Association (1975) Official Handbook.

Mary Muldowney (2006) New Opportunities for Irish Women. Employment in Britain during the Second World War, University of Sussex Journal of Contemporary History, 10.

Tracey (Higgins) Terry, From Ballindine to Barnsley and Beyond (Tales of an Irish Nurse); Birmingham City Archives.

Index

A
Able-bodied, 15-17, 20, 44, 47, 57
Accident Hospital, 26, 74, 82
Accident and Emergency Department, 78, 82, 83, 87
Admissions and Discharges, 26, 56
Arkell Daniel, 58
Assistant Nurses, 41, 47
Aston Poor Law Union, 23, 27, 28, 52

B
Bacon Professor Paul, 81
Beveridge William, 71
Birmingham Area Health Authority, 74
Birmingham City Council, 24, 29, 68
Birmingham General Hospital, 26, 58, 74
Birmingham Children's Hospital, 74, 94
Birmingham Poor Law Union, 23, 24, 27-29, 52, 67
Birmingham Regional Hospital Board, 73, 74
Birmingham University, 81, 82, 130
Blatchford Dr. Raymond, 80, 115
Bodley Miss Amy, 101, 109
Bradbeer Sir Albert, 73, 77, 131
British Medical Journal, 48

C
Casual Wards, 32, 35, 37, 49-56, 73
Census 1881, 21, 22, 38, 39
Census 1901, 21, 22, 38, 39, 64
Chamberlain Joseph, 16
Chapel, 75, 133.
Christmas, 43, 46, 49, 117, 124, 129-130
Commission of Inquiry 1832, 15

Coronary Care, 81
Cowan Miss Mina G., 62

D
Defence Medicine (The Royal Centre for), 82, 84
Dixon Bridget, 75
Dudley Road Hospital, 23, 24, 28, 52, 67, 81

E
E Block, 32, 36, 37, 75, 78, 79, 82, 127, 130
Education, 17, 24, 25
Elizabethan Poor Law 1601, 13
Elliot's Patent Shearing, 30
Ellis Dr. F.W., 27, 65, 67, 68
Eye Department, 115

F
F Block, 37, 75, 78, 79, 94
Friends of Selly Oak Hospital, 75, 115, 133

G
Gerontology, 116
Gibbs William Harvey, 33
Guardians of the Poor, 15-19, 22, 24, 27, 29, 31, 33, 41, 44, 46, 47, 57, 65, 67, 68

H
HSSU Hospital Sterile Supply Unit, 80, 112
Harry Payne Pavilion, 126

Index

Higgs Mary, 51
Hollinshead Dr. Francis, 40, 41, 42, 63
Holmes Edward, 31
Hora Dr. Julian, 40-42, 63

I
Imbeciles, 39, 65
Infectious Diseases, 23, 24, 32, 33, 57
Isaacs Professor Bernard, 81
Insurance, 25
Isolation, 23, 33, 34, 61, 65

J
J Block, 35-37, 75, 78, 79, 100
Jones Miss Agnes, 48

K
K Block, 31, 32, 36, 37, 68, 75, 78, 79, 81, 93, 117, 130, 133
Kelly's Directories, 30, 40, 52
Kelman Mr. R.P.S., 69, 75, 131
King's Norton Poor Law Union, 11, 17, 18, 21, 23- 27, 30, 31, 38, 48, 52, 58

L
L Block, 35, 37, 78, 79, 94
Lady Almoner, 69
Lancet The, 47
Laundry, 35, 51, 62, 68, 75, 128
Little Bromwich Hospital, 73, 104
Local Government Acts, 29, 74
Local Government Board, 16, 48, 60, 62
Loans, 22, 25, 32, 33, 57, 65
Lunatics, 16, 17, 20-23, 26, 39, 52, 57

M
M Block, 35, 37, 43, 78, 79, 116-118
Maternity Services, 61, 63, 68, 79, 91
McVail Dr., 64
Medical Officers, 21, 42, 47, 63, 65, 67
Mental Deficiency Act 1913, 57
Metropolitan Poor Act 1867, 57
Monyhull Colony, 23
Moseley Hall Hospital, 116

N
Nagle Dr. R. E., 81
National Assistance Act 1948, 16
National Health Service Act 1946, 16, 18, 69, 71, 73, 74, 87
National Insurance Act 1911, 16, 28
National Registration Act 1915, 28
New Poor Law 1834, 15, 16, 17, 19, 27, 47, 50, 57, 68
Night Duty, 109-111
Nimptsch Uli, 77
Nurses' Training, 62, 67, 75, 95, 101-114
Nurses' Wages, 48, 62, 106, 113
Nursing Care, 64, 95, 96, 106-108

O
Oakum Picking, 53, 54
Oaklands Nurses' Home, 54, 65
Old Age Pensions Act 1908, 16, 28
Old Poor Law 1601, 13
Ordnance Survey Map 1884, 30, 32, 33
Ordnance Survey Map 1904, 31, 33, 52, 59, 60
Orphans, 16, 17, 22, 38, 64
Outdoor Relief, 15, 19-22, 26, 43
Out-Patient Department, 67, 77, 78, 98, 115

P
Parishes, 13-15, 17, 18, 30
Pathology Department, 67, 78
Pauper Classes, 44
Pauper Inmates Discharge and Regulation Act 1871, 50
Phelps Lieutenant General, 58-60, 65, 68
Physiotherapy, 67, 68, 75, 78, 82
Poor Law Amendment Act 1834 (New Poor Law), 15-17, 19, 28, 46, 47, 50, 57, 68
Poor Law Commissioners, 17, 26, 41, 45, 46, 50
Poor Law Medical Officers' Association, 64
Poor Law Unions, 15, 17, 23, 25, 28, 50-52
Porter Professor Sir Keith, 82
Princess Elizabeth, 131, 132
Public Health, 17, 23, 24
Public Assistance, 29, 52

Q
Queen Elizabeth Hospital, 9, 11, 68, 69, 72, 74, 75, 79, 81, 82, 102, 134

R
Rates Property, 17, 19, 24, 25, 27, 58
Rating and Valuation Act 1925, 29
Registration of Births, Deaths and Marriages, 17, 25, 28, 63
Rheumatology, 81
Royal Orthopaedic Hospital, 75, 78

S
S Block, 80, 82
Sage Mr. Robert, 80
Selly Oak Hospital
   Food, 63, 64, 90, 91, 96
   Doctors, 115, 119
   Maids, 104, 121
   Operating Theatres, 60, 65, 68, 76, 80, 110-112, 119
   Patients, 90-92, 95-96
   Porters, 62, 69, 117, 122, 123
   Visiting, 99, 100
   Ward Blocks, 65-68, 79, 112
   Ward Clerks, 97
Settlement, 14, 19, 21, 26
Sharpe The Rev. C., 42
Shenley Fields Cottage Homes, 22, 26, 39
Sick Poor, 14, 20, 45, 47, 56, 57
Smokey Joe's, 125
Social Club, 124
Springfields Nurses' Home, 101, 113, 131
Stone Breaking, 44, 54

T
Teasedale Miss Joan, 80
Timmins James, 48
Tramps, 9, 19, 28, 32, 35, 49-56

U
Uniforms, 88, 103, 104, 121, 122
University Hospital Birmingham, 74, 82

V
Vaccination, 23, 42
Vagrants, 45, 49-56
Veitch Mr. T.N., 75

W
Walter Joseph, 35
West Heath Hospital, 116
West Lodge/Gateway, 35, 37, 43, 80, 89, 122
West Midlands Regional Health Authority, 74
West Midlands Rehabilitation Centre, 65
Widows, 16, 19, 20, 21, 39
Woodlands Nurses' Home, 65, 67, 101-105, 124, 133
Workhouse
   Casual Wards, 32, 35, 37, 49-56, 73
   Clothes, 44, 53
   Conditions, 15, 16, 18, 38, 44, 47, 53
   Food, 45, 46, 51, 63
   Infirmary, 32, 47, 48, 57-68
   Inmate Classification, 44
   Master/Matron, 32, 35, 39, 39-42
   Merit Ward, 46
   Nurses, 40-42, 47, 62
   Officials, 39-42, 52, 63
   Porters, 35, 40-43, 89
   Routine, 44
   Rules and Regulations, 15-17, 20, 41, 43, 61
   Work, 35, 44, 50, 52-54, 56
World War I, 28, 51, 67
World War II, 69, 94

X
X-Ray Department, 67, 78, 119